MOVIE POSTERS
75 YEARS OF
ACADEMY AWARD®
WINNERS

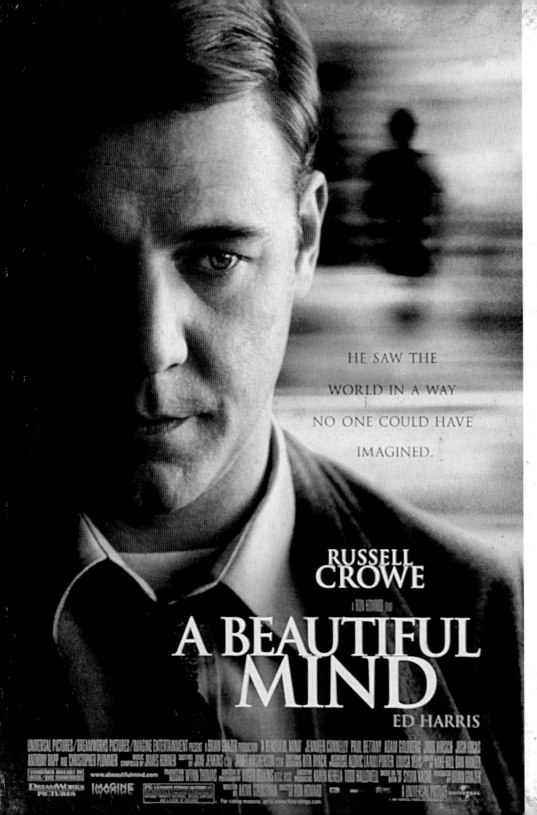

HE SAW THE

WORLD IN A WAY

NO ONE COULD HAVE

IMAGINED.

RUSSELL CROWE

A BEAUTIFUL MIND

ED HARRIS

Library of Congress Cataloging-in-Publication Data

Everett, Diana DiFranco.
    Movie Posters: 75 Years of Academy Award winners/by Diana DiFranco
Everett and Morris Everett, Jr.
        p. cm.
    ISBN 0-7643-1789-X
1. Film posters, American—Catalogs. 2. Academy Awards (Motion
pictures) I. Everett, Morris, 1940 II. Title.
PN1995.9.P5 E84 2002
016.79143'75—dc21

2002152338

Designed by John P. Cheek
Cover design by Bruce M. Waters
Type set in Busorama Md BT/Korinna BT

ISBN: 0-7643-1789-X
Printed in China
1 2 3 4

Published by Schiffer Publishing Ltd.
4880 Lower Valley Road
Atglen, PA 19310
Phone: (610) 593-1777; Fax: (610) 593-2002
E-mail: Schifferbk@aol.com
Please visit our web site catalog at **www.schifferbooks.com**
We are always looking for people to write books on new and related subjects. If you have an
idea for a book please contact us at the above address.

This book may be purchased from the publisher.
Include $3.95 for shipping.
Please try your bookstore first.
You may write for a free catalog.

In Europe, Schiffer books are distributed by
Bushwood Books
6 Marksbury Ave.
Kew Gardens
Surrey TW9 4JF England
Phone: 44 (0) 20 8392-8585; Fax: 44 (0) 20 8392-9876
E-mail: Bushwd@aol.com
Free postage in the U.K., Europe; air mail at cost.

MOVIE POSTERS
75 YEARS OF
ACADEMY AWARD®
WINNERS

DIANA DIFRANCO EVERETT
AND
MORRIS EVERETT, JR.

with Forewords by
Gene Arnold & Mike Hawks

Schiffer Publishing Ltd

4880 Lower Valley Road, Atglen, PA 19310 USA

DEDICATION

We dedicate this book to Alice Ghostley and
Felice Orlandi of stage, screen, and television.

Alice Ghostley in television's hit series,
Designing Women

Alice Ghostley accepts the Best
Actress Oscar for absentee Maggie
Smith ("The Prime of Miss Jean
Brodie," 1968)

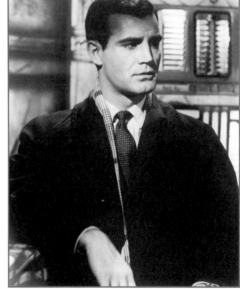

Felice Orlandi in "The Pusher," 1960.

Felice Orlandi in "Bullitt," 1968

CONTENTS

ACKNOWLEDGMENTS

We have so many people to thank for their knowledge, assistance, and support in putting this book together, including: Gene Arnold, Douglas Congdon-Martin, Bruce Davis, Bridget Drago, Morris Everett III, Elizabeth Everett, Rod Flauhaus, Sam Gill, David Graveen, Mike Hawks, Bruce Hershenson, Ron Harvey, Jim Kohler, Peter J. Krembs, The Last Moving Picture Company, Andrea Livingston (The Academy of Motion Picture Arts and Sciences Center for Motion Picture Study), Bruce and Barbara MacArthur, The Margaret Herrick Library of the Academy of Motion Picture Arts and Sciences, Linda Mehr, Scott Miller, Mel Neuhaus (research and photo expertise – couldn't have done it without him!), Mike Orlando, Alice Ours (editing), Adam Ours (computer assistance), John Ours, Jr. (computer consultant and technical advisor), Diana Rezaee for tremendous encouragement, Peter Schiffer, and Melissa Yowken (research and photos).

Morris wishes to make special mention of the following: Steve Schmitz, who showed him his movie poster collection in 1960; Movie Star News in New York City, where he bought his first photo of Natalie Wood in "Splendor in the Grass" from Irving and Paula Klaus in 1961; Publix Book Store in Cleveland, Ohio, where he bought his first set of lobby cards in 1962, Buster Keaton in "The General," for $30.00; Grandmother Wilson, who tried to buy his entire movie poster collection in 1973 for $5,000 because she thought it was getting in the way of his life (he is thankful he did not even consider taking her up on it!); and George Jessel, whose collection of 8,000 1925-35 original 8" x 10" glossy still photos became his first collection purchase in 1968.

Diana gives special thanks to all of the teachers in her life; from her early childhood through Wittenberg University in Springfield, Ohio, and then at The University of Virginia in Charlottesville. She gives particular acknowledgement to Amelia Wiltrack Fakner, a lover of books and a teacher of the tenth magnitude, whose creativity, vision, widsom, and expertise left an indelible mark.

Diana and Mo thank their parents, Morris and Eleanor Everett, and Joseph and Jo DiFranco, for giving them every opportunity for success in life. Above all, they thank God for their many blessings, including the opportunity to write this book.

FOREWORDS

GENE ARNOLD

Sometime in the mid-1970s, one of the first movie poster shows was underway. I had been collecting movie posters, lobby cards, and stills since 1966, and was selling some of these for the very first time at this show.

A young man (we were all young back then!) came up to my table to view the lobby cards I had on display. To my surprise, he picked out some lobbies on Westerns, Silents, Comedy, Mystery, Sci-Fi, Horror, Serials, Short Subjects, and Documentaries. He explained matter-of-factly that he was trying to collect movie items on every motion picture ever made. I thought to myself that it was a wonderful idea and a wonderful goal, but it would never happen. There were just too many movies for him to accomplish that. I believed, after a year or so, he would be disheartened and give up that noble effort. A lesser person would have done just that. But not that young man, not Morris Everett, Jr. (or as he is known to his friends – Morrie).

Unlike most collectors who turn around and sell their acquisitions, Morrie has kept all of his. And what a collection it is! I should know, because over the years I have sent him every obscure title I have ever had. Now Morrie has most every well-known title there is, and has cornered the market on films that were little known, including those from 1930s poverty row companies and other studios that have long since been forgotten.

Morrie may never have a poster-related item on every film ever made – but he'll come close – so close, it's mind-boggling.

That's why when I heard that Morrie and his lovely wife, Diana, were putting together the ultimate Academy Award® book, I knew it would be done right. No one else could compile these images for this book.

Morrie and Diana know movies and their knowledge and their pictures make this a must for all movie afficionados all over the world.

P.S. I know that this won't matter to the purchaser of this book – but they also happen to be some of the nicest people around. Knowledge, niceness, and an inventory of movie paper – what a combination!

Gene Arnold always wanted to be a broadcaster. After graduating from the University of Houston in 1959, that's immediately what he did. He worked as a disc jockey, newscaster and sportscaster, broadcasting everything from wrestling to the Houston Oilers (now the Tennessee Titans). For ten years he broadcast the games of the now defunct Southwest Conference.

It was during this time that Arnold was first introduced to movie posters. He was quickly addicted, as most collectors are.

After leaving broadcasting, he bought out a famous poster and still shop called Film Favorites. He later changed the name to Arnold Movie Poster Company, and after the internet emerged on the world scene, changed it once again to MoviePosters.com.

Arnold is president of this worldwide internet company and devotes all of his time to its operation from its home base of Tomball, outside of Houston, Texas.

He is married to Laurel, his wife of 38 years, and has three grown children.

MIKE HAWKS

When I first met Morris Everett in the mid-1970s, he told me his goal was to get at least one lobby card for every movie ever made. Needless to say, I tried my best to humor him at the time. Now, over twenty-five years later, here I am writing about him and his collection. I, like Morris, have been collecting lobby cards for over thirty years and, while I have over four thousand cards, he has acquired cards from over thirty-seven thousand movies! Needless to say, he is a very serious collector.

I had been invited over the years to come to Ohio and look at his personal collection. I finally decided to do so and, after arriving, found myself face to face with many file cabinets filled to the brim with goodies. Although my main interest was to see what he had in pre-1920 lobbies, it still took me eight days to complete my journey. Yes, I saw everything from *Aaron Loves Angela* to *Zulu,* and from *Metropolis* and *Gone With the Wind* to *Jungle Jim on Pygmy Island.* Obviously, when one starts a collection of this magnitude, he must take the good with the bad, and the wonderful to the truly terrible!

Morris is a leader in collecting circles. With not only the largest and best collection of its kind in the Universe, but also with the rare good fortune to have found his wife, Diana…a woman whom I feel is different from many wives and girlfriends who only humor their collecting partners. She understands and appreciates what he is doing. And what good fortune for us that they have decided to preserve movie history so that we and future generations can see the development of movies as an art form. I look forward, as you will, to turning the pages of this book on a great industry and a great collection.

Mike Hawks and his collection are the subject of two books, Lobby Cards: The Classic Films, *and* Lobby Cards: The Classic Comedies. *He is affiliated with Larry Edmunds Book Shop, Inc. in Hollywood, California, which offers the world's largest collection of books on cinema.*

AUTHORS' NOTE

I have been collecting for forty-one years, and have amassed the largest collection of movie lobby cards and posters in the world. There are more than 37,000 titles and 120,000 different pieces. I have also collected more than two million photos and slides of the entertainment business from 1910 to present. Collecting all of these items has been a life-long passion and now some of them can be shared in this book.

My wife and best friend, Diana, makes this book a reality. Without her support and assistance this book (and the others I have in mind!) would not have happened. Her wisdom, her writing and editing skills, and her computer skills were essential. We are co-authors in the truest sense. Thank you, Diana!

— Morrie

I met my husband many years ago, but our first date was at Cinecon 25 in Cleveland, which he chaired, in September of 1989. At that time, I did not know a half-sheet from a bed sheet…but now movie poster lingo is a part of my work and my daily life. I have always had a fascination with the entertainment world, having Alice Ghostley and Felice Orlandi as my aunt and uncle. I attended exciting events in New York and Hollywood while growing up, and visited the homes of their friends, including Paul Lynde, Jonathan Winters, Charles Nelson Reilly, and more. But on that wonderful and memorable first date with Morris almost fifteen years ago, I met both Porky and Butch of the Little Rascals, Joan Bennett, and many collectors and dealers in movie memorabilia whom I now look forward to seeing at various times and places throughout the year. Each year in Columbus, Ohio, we regroup at Cinevent, but this time the whole family and several special friends work together to put on the Vintage Movie Poster Art Auction in conjunction with that event. To be sure, one cannot be married to Morris Everett, Jr. without having every aspect of movies be a part of daily life! From Roy Rogers and Dale Evans and Hopalong Cassidy posters in our family room (I got to choose those!), to running an internet movie memorabilia business (we are both LASTMO & LMPC on eBay), my life is irrevocably entwined with the buying, selling, trading, and collecting of movie memorabilia. I love the posters, stills, and lobbies, and I value the friendship of our colleagues in this fascinating business/hobby.

– Diana

We are always on the lookout for poster and photo images that we do not have. We also have over 100,000 posters and lobby cards for sale, and we buy, sell, and trade daily. We welcome your input, and your communications by email to lastmo@aol.com, by phone to 440-256-3660, or by mail to The Last Moving Picture Company, 10535 Chillicothe Road, Kirtland, Ohio, 44094. Our website is www.vintagefilmposters.com.

– Morris Everett, Jr.
– Diana DiFranco Everett

INTRODUCTION

March 23, 2003 marks the 75th Anniversary of the Academy Awards ®. The following pages will chronicle those years using poster, lobby card, and photo images. For us and for our readers there is no subject more exciting and interesting.

The definitive Oscar ® book by Robert Osborne (*70 Years of the Oscar* ®), is filled with so many little known facts: the number of awards, how they were added or dropped over the years, and their criteria. It is an amazing history. As we read the book and analyzed each award year, we realized that there were lobby cards, posters, or stills made for these films. The perfect material for a book such as this!

This book contains primarily lobby cards, which are in fact posters. A lobby card, which usually came in sets of eight, is considered one of the smallest posters made for each film. The earliest known lobby cards are dated 1913, and are 8" x 10" or 11" x 14" in size. In those days and until the early 1920s, it was not uncommon for there to have been sets of lobby cards made in both sizes for each film. The earliest lobbies were two-color varieties. These were followed by sepia-toned cards and, then, hand-colored. By the late 1920s, there were beautiful full-color lobby cards and stone-lithographed posters that, today, are highly sought-after. Often the border-art showed a strong Art Deco influence that is as interesting as the movie image!

In the glory days of poster advertising, a theater could order the following-sized posters from a poster exchange:

Mini window card – vertical, 9" x 14":
Set of eight lobby cards – horizontal, 11" x 14"
Set of eight jumbo lobby cards – vertical or horizontal, 14" x 17"
Window card – vertical , 14" x 22"
Jumbo window card – vertical, 22" x 28"
Half-sheet – horizontal, 22" x 28"
Insert – vertical, 14" x 36"
One-sheet – vertical, 27" x 41"
British Quad – approx. 30" x 40"
Three-sheet – vertical (three or four pieces), 41" x 81"
Six-sheet – horizontal (four pieces), 81" x 81"
Twenty-four sheet (twelve pieces), various billboard sizes
French, German, Spanish, and Mexican Lobby cards – various sizes

Exceptions to the above measurements and quantities exist in the form of larger lobby card sets (4, 9, 10, 12, 14, and 16 card sets), door panels, eight-sheets, and oversize banners.

Today, movie posters are sold by well-known auction houses. The world record price was set a few years ago when a one-sheet poster of Boris Karloff in "The Mummy" (1932) sold, with buyer's premium, for $460,000. Not bad, for a poster a theater would buy for fifty cents in 1932! Posters were often rented from and returned to the studios. They were torn, taped, pin-holed, lost, destroyed, and generally not collected or kept (until the 1950s). There are some features, one-reels, shorts, cartoons, and documentaries for which there is no known "paper" in existence. Others, especially cartoons, were unavailable for inclusion in this book. Every effort has been made to identify the images of early principal and supporting players, but some identifications have escaped us. We welcome any information our readers may provide for future editions and updates; we would like very much to recognize and remember these early actors and actresses for the sake of film history.

Finally, a word about the current state of movie poster collecting and values! Academy Award ® posters, especially one-sheets, are among the most highly sought-after and valuable. Several of the early award posters are worth more than $20,000. Years ago, Morris presented The Academy with the one-sheet for the movie "Wings," which now hangs in their gallery. The value of this poster, an only known copy, would be near fifty thousand or more dollars today! Though they have been challenged for saying the following, the authors truly believe that movie posters have outperformed gold, stamps, coins, sports trading cards, comic books, and the stock market with never a down side! We have seen steady growth over these past forty years; for example, an Errol Flynn photo (from "The Adventures of Robin Hood"), purchased for twenty-five cents in 1962, is now worth twenty dollars. A lobby card of Boris Karloff in "The Mummy," purchased for five hundred dollars in 1985, is now worth ten thousand dollars. Very little has gone down in value.

There are conventions, auctions, periodicals, price guides, websites, stores, galleries, exhibits, articles, and more which deal with the values of movie memorabilia. The values in our price guide accompanying this book may seem high to some, but often the image shown is the best card out of a set of eight. Important factors in choosing which lobby card to select from a set include condition, image, and whether or not it is the title card, which is usually the most valuable card in the set. Cards representing an Academy Award® winning actor or actress are also prized.

1927-1928

WINGS
Paramount Famous Lasky

- **Best Picture:** Produced by Lucien Hubbard.
- **Engineering Effects:** Roy Pomeroy

In this lobby card, Red Cross nurse Clara Bow looks wistfully at Buddy Rogers, as he smiles at fellow World War I airman Richard Arlen.

SUNRISE
Fox

- **Unique and Artistic Picture**
- **Cinematography:** Charles Rosher and Karl Struss

Farmer George O'Brien plots with Margaret Livingston to kill his wife (Janet Gaynor).

THE LAST COMMAND
Paramount Famous Lasky

- **Best Actor:** Emil Jannings

Emil Jannings, a former Russian general, became a Hollywood actor and is seen here with Evelyn Brent. Jannings won the Best Actor award for his work in two different films, both pictured here.

THE WAY OF ALL FLESH
Paramount Famous Lasky

- **Best Actor:** Emil Jannings

Emil Jannings plays the role of a brooding immigrant (Dutch).

7TH HEAVEN
Fox

- **Best Actress:** Janet Gaynor
- **Direction (Dramatic Picture):** Frank Borzage
- **Writing (Adaptation):** Benjamin Glazer

In this title lobby card, Janet Gaynor meets her love, Charles Farrell, on the roof. Gaynor won her award for two different films, both pictured here.

STREET ANGEL
Fox

- **Best Actress:** Janet Gaynor

Charles Farrell gazes adoringly at ballerina Janet Gaynor in the gypsy wagon.

Two Arabian Knights

The Caddo Company, United Artists

- **Direction (Comedy Picture):** Lewis Milestone

William Boyd (left) and Louis Wolheim (right) ogle harem queen Mary Astor.

Underworld

Paramount Famous Lasky

- **Writing (Original Story):** Ben Hecht

Clive Brook attacks George Bancroft as he hugs Evelyn Brent.

- **Writing (Title Writing):** Joseph Farnham

The Dove

Joseph M. Schenck Productions, United Artists

- **Art Direction:** William Cameron Menzies

Croupier Eddie Borden warns Gilbert Roland, as he embraces Norma Talmadge.

Tempest

Art Cinema, United Artists

- **Art Direction:** William Cameron Menzies

Princess Camilla Horn scorns Sergeant John Barrymore during the Russian Revolution.

This wonderful lobby card has it all! Al Jolson sings "Mammy" in the border art of the lobby card for this part-talkie, and is also shown holding May McAvoy, while chorus girls strain to have their faces seen.

THE JAZZ SINGER
Warner Brothers

- **Special Award:** Warner Brothers for outstanding talking picture.

THE CIRCUS
United Artists

- **Special Award:** Charles Chaplin for directing, producing, and writing this film.

Charlie Chaplin falls in love with bareback rider Merna Kennedy.

1928-1929

THE BROADWAY MELODY
M-G-M

- **Best Picture:** Produced by Harry Rapf

Sisters Anita Page and Bessie Love compete for the love of showman Charles King.

IN OLD ARIZONA
Fox

- **Best Actor:** Warner Baxter

Edmund Lowe and Dorothy Burgess share grapes in this first western talkie!

COQUETTE
United Artists

- **Best Actress:** Mary Pickford

Flapper Mary Pickford strives to explain that Johnny Mack Brown is her choice.

THE DIVINE LADY
First National

- **Direction:** Frank Lloyd

In this title card, a pensive Corinne Griffith and a triumphant Victor Varconi are shown with a host of cheering pirates.

THE PATRIOT
Paramount Famous Lasky

- **Writing:** Hans Kraly

A quiet moment for Neil Hamilton and Florence Vidor in this Ernst Lubitsch classic.

WHITE SHADOWS IN THE SOUTH SEAS
Cosmopolitan, M-G-M

- **Cinematography:** Clyde De Vinna

Monte Blue (center) plays with the braids of South Seas lovely Raquel Torres, while a criminal type looks on.

THE BRIDGE OF SAN LUIS REY
M-G-M

- **Art Direction:** Cedric Gibbons

Lily Damita plays the social climbing temptress in this part-silent, part-talkie feature.

1929-1930

ALL QUIET ON THE WESTERN FRONT
Universal

- **Best Picture:** Produced by Carl Laemmle, Jr.
- **Direction:** Lewis Milestone

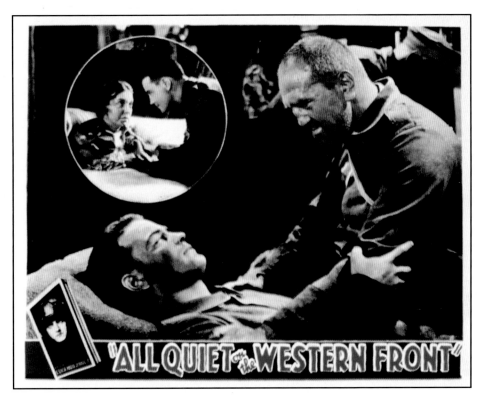

Inset of Lew Ayres with mother Beryl Mercer; and Lew again in a scene with Louis Wolheim, as inexperienced German soldiers in World War I.

DISRAELI
Warner Brothers

- **Best Actor:** George Arliss

George Arliss (right) as British Prime Minister Disraeli, grabs the arm of Anthony Bushell, who is enamored of Joan Bennett. Arliss won this award for two different films, both pictured here.

THE GREEN GODDESS
Warner Brothers

- **Best Actor:** George Arliss

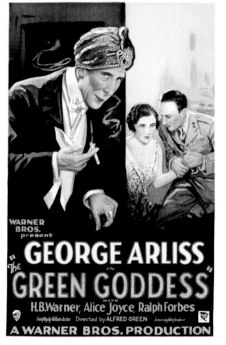

In this remake of his 1923 silent film, George Arliss holds Alice Joyce and H.B. Warner captive.

THE DIVORCEE
M-G-M

- **Best Actress:** Norma Shearer

Conrad Nagel romances divorcee Norma Shearer. Shearer won this award for two different films, both pictured here.

THEIR OWN DESIRE
M-G-M

- **Best Actress:** Norma Shearer

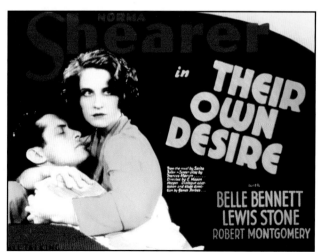

Norma Shearer and Robert Montgomery pursue their desire on this Title Card.

THE BIG HOUSE
Cosmopolitan, M-G-M

- **Writing:** Frances Marion
- **Sound Recording:** Douglas Shearer

Wallace Beery threatens Chester Morris with a shiv in this film about an attempted prison escape, in which almost everyone dies!

WITH BYRD AT THE SOUTH POLE
Paramount Publix

- **Cinematography:** Joseph T. Rucker and Willard Van Der Veer

Rear Admiral Byrd leads an expedition to the Antarctic South Pole.

KING OF JAZZ
Universal

- **Art Direction:** Herman Rosse

This musical extravaganza is dominated, for the most part, by Paul Whiteman's band.

1930-1931

CIMARRON
RKO Radio

- **Best Picture:** Produced by William LeBaron
- **Writing (Adaptation):** Howard Estabrook
- **Art Direction:** Max Ree

A FREE SOUL
M-G-M

- **Best Actor:** Lionel Barrymore

Norma Shearer, daughter of lawyer Barrymore, falls in love with gangster Clark Gable.

MIN AND BILL
M-G-M

- **Best Actress:** Marie Dressler

Richard Dix contemplates use of his six-shooters as a fearful Irene Dunne looks on.

Love on the waterfront between two old timers, Marie Dressler and Wallace Beery.

Skippy
Paramount Publix

- **Direction:** Norman Taurog

Mitzi Green is teased by Jackie Cooper, Robert Coogan, and Jackie Searl.

The Dawn Patrol
Warner Brothers- First National

- **Writing (Original Story):** John Monk Saunders

Pilot Douglas Fairbanks, Jr. talks with fellow World War I ace Richard Barthelmess.

Tabu
Paramount Publix

- **Cinematography:** Floyd Crosby

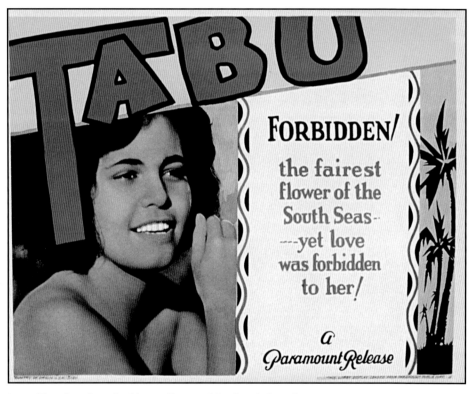

Anna Chevalier plays the "fairest flower of the South Seas."

- **Sound Recording:** Paramount Publix Studio Sound Department

1931-1932

GRAND HOTEL
M-G-M

- **Best Picture:** Produced by Irving Thalberg

This terrific cast makes the dramatic story of two days in a Berlin hotel believable. Left to right: Greta Garbo, John Barrymore, Joan Crawford, Wallace Beery, and Lionel Barrymore.

THE CHAMP
M-G-M

- **Best Actor:** Wallace Beery
- **Writing (Original Story):** Frances Marion

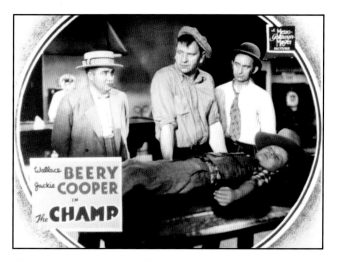

Edward Brophy looks to Wallace Beery and Roscoe Ates for guidance on how to deal with little Jackie Cooper.

DR. JEKYLL AND MR. HYDE
Paramount Publix

- **Best Actor:** Fredric March

Mr. Hyde (Fredric March) menaces Halliwell Hobbes. At right, Dr. Jekyll remains aloof.

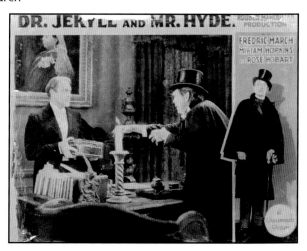

THE SIN OF MADELON CLAUDET
M-G-M

- **Best Actress:** Helen Hayes

Lewis Stone romances Helen Hayes in this tearjerker.

BAD GIRL
Fox

- **Direction:** Frank Borzage
- **Writing:** Edwin Burke

A sentimental New York City love story in which William Pawley, Sally Eilers, and Minna Gombell are the stars.

SHANGHAI EXPRESS
Paramount Publix

- **Cinematography:** Lee Garmes

Eugene Pallette, Anna May Wong, Marlene Dietrich, and Clive Brook join together to take on Chinese warlords.

TRANSATLANTIC
Fox

- **Art Direction:** Gordon Wiles

Lois Moran holds her father, Jean Hersholt, protectively as Edmund Lowe intervenes.

- **Sound Recording:** Paramount Publix Studio Sound Department

FLOWERS AND TREES
Disney, United Artists

- **Short Subject:** Cartoon

Our hero, the good tree, tickles the tummy of the bad tree!

THE MUSIC BOX
M-G-M

- **Short Subject:** Hal Roach

Oliver Hardy and Stan Laurel in another fine mess!

WRESTLING SWORDFISH
Mack Sennett, Educational

- **Short Subject:** Novelty

- **Special Award:** for the creation of Mickey Mouse, to Walt Disney

Rare Title Card showing an early Mickey Mouse.

1932-1933

CAVALCADE
Fox

- **Best Picture:** Winfield Sheehan, Studio Head
- **Direction:** Frank Lloyd
- **Art Direction:** William S. Darling

THE PRIVATE LIFE OF HENRY VIII
London Films, United Artists (British)

- **Best Actor:** Charles Laughton

Robert Donat appreciates Binnie Barnes….and so does Charles (Henry VIII) Laughton!

Clive Brook and Diana Wynyard are the leads in this film about how Londoners were affected by World War I.

MORNING GLORY
RKO Radio

- **Best Actress:** Katharine Hepburn

A stage struck Katharine Hepburn gazes at Adolphe Menjou, while a concerned Douglas Fairbanks, Jr. and a smiling C. Aubrey Smith look on.

LITTLE WOMEN
RKO Radio

- **Writing (Adaptation):** Victor Heerman and Sarah Y. Mason

Katharine Hepburn, Jean Parker, Joan Bennett, and Frances Dee as the stars of this Louisa May Alcott classic story.

ONE WAY PASSAGE
Warner Brothers

- **Writing (Original Story):** Robert Lord

Joe Sawyer points his pistol at William Powell in this shipboard detective story.

A FAREWELL TO ARMS
Paramount

- **Cinematography:** Charles Bryant Lang, Jr.
- **Sound Recording:** Franklin B. Hansen, Sound Director, Paramount Studio Sound Department

Soldier Gary Cooper is introduced to nurse Helen Hayes by Adolphe Menjou and Mary Philips in this World War I story set in Italy.

THE THREE LITTLE PIGS
Disney, United Artists

• **Short Subject:** Cartoon

This Spanish lobby card shows the practical pig instructing his brothers how to build a house.

SO THIS IS HARRIS
Louis Brock, RKO Radio. (Special)

• **Short Subject:** Comedy

It looks like everyone is waving at Harris.

• **Assistant Director:** (New Category)
    William Tummel: Fox
    Charles Dorian: M-G-M
    Charles Barton: Paramount
    Dewey Starkey: RKO Radio
    Fred Fox: United Artists
    Scott Beal: Universal
    Gordon Hollingshead: Warner Brothers

KRAKATOA
Joe Rock, Educational. (Three-reel Special)

• **Short Subject:** Novelty

This one-sheet tells it all: total volcano eruption!

1934

IT HAPPENED ONE NIGHT
Columbia

- **Best Picture:** Produced by Harry Cohn
- **Best Actor:** Clark Gable
- **Best Actress:** Claudette Colbert
- **Direction:** Frank Capra
- **Writing (Adaptation):** Robert Riskin

MANHATTAN MELODRAMA
Cosmopolitan, M-G-M

- **Writing (Original Story):** Arthur Caesar

Clark Gable, Myrna Loy, and William Powell juggle crime, law and order, friendship, and love in this melodrama.

CLEOPATRA
Paramount

- **Cinematography:** Victor Milner

Famous couple Clark Gable and Claudette Colbert pose for this lovely portrait lobby card.

Warren William (Caesar) and a sultry Claudette Colbert (Cleopatra).

THE MERRY WIDOW
M-G-M

- **Art Direction:** Cedric Gibbons and Frederic Hope

In a Cinderella-like setting, Maurice Chevalier puts the slipper on Jeanette MacDonald's foot.

ONE NIGHT OF LOVE
Columbia

- **Sound Recording:** John Livadary, Sound Director, Columbia Studio Sound Department
- **Music (Score):** Louis Silvers. Thematic music by Victor Schertzinger and Gus Kahn.

Grace Moore, opera star, sings popular music and opera with Tullio Carminati.

ESKIMO
M-G-M

- **Film Editing** (new category): Conrad Nevig

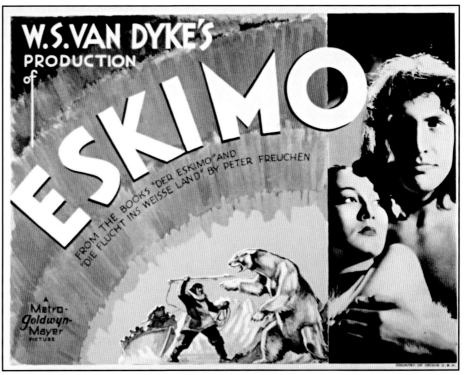

Real Eskimos, Lotus Long and Mala, starred in this almost-documentary film.

THE GAY DIVORCEE
RKO Radio

- **Music (Song):** "The Continental." Music by Con Conrad. Lyrics by Herb Magidson.

Colorful artwork on this title card shows Ginger Rogers and Fred Astaire ready to dance.

VIVA VILLA!
M-G-M

- **Assistant Director:** John Waters

Stu Erwin tries to stare down Wallace Beery (Villa), who restrains Leo Carrillo from shooting.

THE TORTOISE AND THE HARE
Disney, United Artists

- **Short Subject:** Cartoon

The hare was certain he would win, but was passed at the finish line by the determined tortoise.

La Cucaracha
RKO Radio

- **Short Subject:** Comedy

This musical, starring Don Alvarado, was Vincente Minnelli's favorite, consequently influencing all of his musical direction in the future.

City of Wax
Educational

- **Short Subject:** Battle for Life Series

- **Special Award:** Shirley Temple, for outstanding film work in 1934.

A nice portrait of Adolphe Menjou and Shirley Temple !

1935

MUTINY ON THE BOUNTY
M-G-M

- **Best Picture:** Produced by Irving Thalberg with Albert Lewin

Fletcher Christian (Clark Gable) is not going to take orders from Captain Bligh (Charles Laughton).

THE INFORMER
RKO Radio

- **Best Actor:** Victor McLaglen
- **Direction:** John Ford
- **Writing (Screenplay):** Dudley Nichols
- **Music (Score):** Max Steiner, RKO Radio Music Dept.

Heather Angel accuses Victor McLaglen while Joe Sawyer and Preston Foster judge him.

DANGEROUS
Warner Brothers

- **Best Actress:** Bette Davis

One of the most beautiful Bette Davis title cards. She looks dangerous.

THE SCOUNDREL
Paramount

- **Writing (Original Story):** Ben Hecht and Charles MacArthur

Noel Coward seems to be having trouble choosing between Julie Haydon and Hope Williams.

A MIDSUMMER NIGHT'S DREAM
Warner Brothers

- **Cinematography:** Hal Mohr
- **Film Editing:** Ralph Dawson

Puck (Mickey Rooney) laughs at Olivia de Havilland as she stars in her first film.

THE DARK ANGEL
Goldwyn, United Artists

- **Art Direction:** Richard Day

Three life long friends, Merle Oberon, Herbert Marshall, and Fredric March have a tragic ending.

NAUGHTY MARIETTA
M-G-M

- **Sound Recording:** Douglas Shearer, Sound Director, M-G-M Studio Sound Dept.

Light opera stars Jeanette MacDonald and Nelson Eddy sing their way across the screen in this period piece.

THE LIVES OF A BENGAL LANCER
Paramount

- **Assistant Director:** Clem Beauchamp and Paul Wing

Franchot Tone, Gary Cooper, and Sir Guy Standing exchange pleasantries with J. Carrol Naish, while secretly hating each other.

GOLD DIGGERS OF 1935
Warner Brothers – First National

- **Music (Song):** "Lullaby of Broadway." Music by Harry Warren. Lyrics by Al Rubin.

Adolphe Menjou is comforted by Alice Brady as tired chorus girls look on.

BROADWAY MELODY OF 1936
M-G-M

- **Dance Direction** (new category): Dave Gould ("I've Got a Feeling You're Fooling")

Eleanor Powell prepares to wow the assembled cast with her dancing and singing abilities.

FOLIES BERGÈRE
20th Century, United Artists

- **Dance Direction:** "Straw Hat" – Dave Gould

Maurice Chevalier charms Ann Sothern.

THREE ORPHAN KITTENS
Disney, United Artists

- **Short Subject:** Cartoon

The three orphan kittens at play.

HOW TO SLEEP
M-G-M (Miniature Series)

- **Short Subject:** Comedy

WINGS OVER MT. EVEREST
Educational

- **Short Subject:** Novelty

1936

THE GREAT ZIEGFELD
M-G-M

- **Best Picture:** Produced by Hunt Stromberg
- **Best Actress:** Luise Rainer
- **Dance Direction:** Seymour Felix for "A Pretty Girl is Like a Melody"

An all-star cast graces this title lobby card: Myrna Loy, William Powell, Luise Rainer, Frank Morgan, Fanny Brice, Virginia Bruce, Harriet Hoctor, and Ray Bolger.

THE STORY OF LOUIS PASTEUR
Warner Brothers

- **Best Actor:** Paul Muni
- **Writing (Original Story):** Pierre Collings and Sheridan Gibney
- **Writing (Screen Play):** Pierre Collings and Sheridan Gibney

Paul Muni, Josephine Hutchinson, and Anita Louise star in this drama about the famous French scientist.

COME AND GET IT
Goldwyn, United Artists

- **Best Supporting Actor:** Walter Brennan

Edward Arnold and Frances Farmer look on as Walter Brennan examines a unique hat.

ANTHONY ADVERSE
Warner Brothers

- **Best Supporting Actress:** Gale Sondergaard
- **Cinematography:** Gaetano Gaudio
- **Film Editing:** Ralph Dawson
- **Music (Score):** Warner Brothers Studio Music Department, Leo Forbstein, head. Score by Eric Wolfgang Korngold.

Claude Rains and Gale Sondergaard plot evil deeds to gain more money and power.

MR. DEEDS GOES TO TOWN
Columbia

- **Direction:** Frank Capra

Nice portrait card of Gary Cooper and Jean Arthur!

DODSWORTH
Goldwyn, United Artists

- **Art Direction:** Richard Day

Walter Huston holds Ruth Chatterton's hands, while Spring Byington smiles at Harlan Briggs.

SAN FRANCISCO
M-G-M

- **Sound Recording:** Douglas Shearer, Sound Director, M-G-M Studio Sound Dept.

Clark Gable and Jeanette MacDonald team up in this musical about San Francisco at the time of the great fire.

SWING TIME
RKO Radio

- **Music (Song):** "The Way You Look Tonight." Music by Jerome Kern. Lyrics by Dorothy Fields.

Ginger Rogers and Fred Astaire, lighting up this lobby card just like they light up the stage when they dance.

THE CHARGE OF THE LIGHT BRIGADE
Warner Brothers

- **Assistant Director:** Jack Sullivan

This linen title card prominently features the images of Errol Flynn and Olivia de Havilland, as well as some art featuring an action scene from the film.

COUNTRY COUSIN
Disney, United Artists

- **Short Subject:** Cartoon

The city cousin meets the country cousin at the city limits, welcoming him for a visit.

BORED OF EDUCATION
Roach, M-G-M

- **Short Subject (One-reel):** Our Gang

THE PUBLIC PAYS
M-G-M

- **Short Subject (Two-reel):** Crime Doesn't Pay Series

GIVE ME LIBERTY
Warner Brothers

- **Short Subject (Color):** Broadway Brevities Series

THE MARCH OF TIME
RKO Radio

- **Special Award:** Newsreels

This 1936 poster is typical of the March of Time Series, which lasted almost ten years.

THE GARDEN OF ALLAH
Selznick International Production

- **Special Award:** Color Cinematography – W. Howard Greene and Harold Rosson.

A troubled Charles Boyer does not appear to be pleased with Basil Rathbone, yet Marlene Dietrich and C. Aubrey Smith look relaxed and happy.

1937

THE LIFE OF EMILE ZOLA
Warner Brothers

- **Best Picture:** Produced by Henry Blanke
- **Best Supporting Actor:** Joseph Schildkraut
- **Writing (Screenplay):** Heinz Herald, Geza Herczeg, and Norman Reilly Raine

Paul Muni (Zola) defends Joseph Schildkraut (Dreyfus) in court.

CAPTAINS COURAGEOUS
M-G-M

- **Best Actor:** Spencer Tracy

Freddie Bartholomew and Spencer Tracy in a naval race. Lionel Barrymore keeps an eye on their rival.

THE GOOD EARTH
M-G-M

- **Best Actress:** Luise Rainer
- **Cinematography:** Karl Freund

Paul Muni and Luise Rainer star in this gripping drama about Chinese farmers struggling to survive, especially against an attack of locusts.

In Old Chicago
20th Century Fox

- **Best Supporting Actress:** Alice Brady
- **Assistant Director:** Robert Webb

Left to right: Tom Brown, Phyllis Brooks, Don Ameche, Alice Brady, and Tyrone Power. This happy scene is from before Alice and the cow started the Chicago fire!

The Awful Truth
Columbia

- **Director:** Leo McCarey

Irene Dunne and Cary Grant get divorced, but seek help from the furry therapist in the middle of this lobby card!

A Star is Born
Selznick, United Artists

- **Writing (Original Story):** William A. Wellman and Robert Carson
- **Special Award:** Color Photography- W. Howard Greene

This classic film was remade three times! Left to right: Janet Gaynor, Fredric March, Adolphe Menjou, Lionel Stander, and unidentified photographer.

WAIKIKI WEDDING
Paramount

- **Music (Song):** "Sweet Leilani." Music and lyrics by Harry Owens

Left to right: Shirley Ross, Bing Crosby, Martha Raye, and Bob Burns star in this musical comedy.

LOST HORIZON
Columbia

- **Art Direction:** Stephen Goosson
- **Film Editing:** Gene Havlick and Gene Milford

Jane Wyatt tries to stop Ronald Colman and Margo from leaving Shangri-la.

100 MEN AND A GIRL
Universal

- **Music (Score):** Charles Previn, head, Universal Studio Music Dept.

Deanna Durbin, flanked by Mischa Auer and Leopold Stokowski on the left; and Adolphe Menjou and Alice Brady on the right.

THE HURRICANE
Goldwyn, United Artists

- **Sound Recording:** Thomas T. Moulton

Jon Hall, Dorothy Lamour, and Mary Astor cook fish over an open fire before the hurricane begins.

A DAMSEL IN DISTRESS
RKO Radio

- **Dance Direction:** "Fun House" – Hermes Pan

Joan Fontaine, Fred Astaire, George Burns, and Gracie Allen combine singing, dancing, and comedy in this musical.

THE OLD MILL
Disney, RKO Radio

- **Short Subject:** Cartoon

The old mill keeps turning while the ducks quack at an unwelcome visitor.

PRIVATE LIFE OF THE GANNETS
Educational

- **Short Subject (One-reel)**

TORTURE MONEY
M-G-M

- **Short Subject (Two-reel):** Crime Doesn't Pay Series

George Lynn, Vernon McCarthy, and Mary Doran discuss the problem.

PENNY WISDOM
M-G-M

- **Short Subject (Color):** Pete Smith Specialties Series

You Can't Take it With You
Columbia

- **Best Picture:** Produced by Frank Capra
- **Direction:** Frank Capra

Boys Town
M-G-M

- **Best Actor:** Spencer Tracy
- **Writing (Original Story):** Eleanore Griffin and Dore Schary

Mickey Rooney portrays a smiling young boy whose life was changed by Father Flanigan (Spencer Tracy) at Boys Town.

That's Frank Capra sitting seventh from left on the fence! Featured prominently at left , top to bottom, are Jean Arthur, Lionel Barrymore, James Stewart, and Edward Arnold. Additional actors on the fence include Ann Miller, Mischa Auer, Spring Byington, Donald Meek, and Eddie "Rochester" Anderson.

JEZEBEL
Warner Brothers

- **Best Actress:** Bette Davis
- **Best Supporting Actress:** Fay Bainter

KENTUCKY
20ᵗʰ Century-Fox

- **Best Supporting Actor:** Walter Brennan

Southern belle Bette Davis flirts with George Brent while Henry Fonda, Margaret Lindsay, Fay Bainter, and Richard Cromwell look on disapprovingly.

Horsebreeder Walter Brennan, Loretta Young, and Richard Greene check out the horses.

PYGMALION
M-G-M

- **Writing:** George Bernard Shaw. Adaptation by Ian Dalrymple, Cecil Lewis, and W.P. Lipscomb.

This Bernard Shaw story starring Leslie Howard and Wendy Hiller is a more serious, nonmusical presentation of "My Fair Lady," which was filmed later.

THE GREAT WALTZ
M-G-M

- **Cinematography:** Joseph Ruttenberg

This musical stars Fernand Gravet, Miliza Korjus, and Luise Rainer.

THE ADVENTURES OF ROBIN HOOD
Warner Brothers

- **Art Direction:** Carl J. Weyl
- **Film Editing:** Ralph Dawson
- **Music (Original Score):** Erich Wolfgang Korngold

Another great linen portrait card, with Olivia de Havilland and Errol Flynn.

The Cowboy and the Lady
Goldwyn, United Artists

- **Sound Recording:** Thomas Moulton, Sound Director, United Artists Studio Sound Dept.

Gary Cooper shows affection for Merle Oberon in this comedy love story.

Big Broadcast of 1938
Paramount

- **Music (Song):** "Thanks for the Memory." Music by Ralph Rainger. Lyrics by Leo Robin.

W.C. Fields terrorizes the caddies in this wonderful comedy.

Alexander's Ragtime Band
20ᵗʰ Century-Fox

- **Best Scoring:** Alfred Newman

Alice Faye, Don Ameche, and Tyrone Power, in their respective roles as singer, composer, and band leader, take musical advice that produces such songs as "Easter Parade" and "Blue Skies" in this film. Note, at far left, comedian Jack Haley before his Oz tin woodman role!

SNOW WHITE AND THE SEVEN DWARFS
Disney

• **Special Award:** Walt Disney, for screen innovation

Hey Grumpy! Join the fun and hang up that stocking!

SWEETHEARTS
M-G-M

• **Special Award:** Color Cinematography – Oliver Marsh and Allen Davey

Nelson Eddy cozies up to Jeanette MacDonald, despite the Hollywood rumor that he had trouble kissing her because she had the habit of chewing garlic.

Spawn of the North
Paramount

- **Special Award:** Special Effects by Gordon Jennings, assisted by Jan Domela, Dev Jennings, Irmin Roberts, and Art Smith. Transparencies by Farciot Edouart, assisted by Loyal Griggs; Sound Effects by Loren Ryder, assisted by Harry Mills, Louis H. Mesenkop, and Walter Oberst.

Dorothy Lamour, Lynne Overman, Henry Fonda, Louise Platt, George Raft, and John Barrymore drink a toast.

Ferdinand the Bull
Disney, RKO Radio

- **Short Subject:** Cartoon

Ferdinand takes time to smell the flowers, preferring to avoid a fight.

That Mothers Might Live
M-G-M

- **Short Subject (One-reel):** Miniature Series

Declaration of Independence
Warner Brothers

- **Short Subject (Two-reel):** Historical Featurette

1939

GONE WITH THE WIND
M-G-M, Selznick

- **Best Picture:** Produced by David O. Selznick
- **Best Actress:** Vivien Leigh
- **Best Supporting Actress:** Hattie McDaniel
- **Direction:** Victor Fleming
- **Film Editing:** Hal C. Kern, and James E. Newcom
- **Art Direction:** Lyle Wheeler
- **Writing (Screenplay):** Sidney Howard
- **Cinematography (Color):** Ernest Haller and Ray Rennahan
- **Special Award:** William Cameron Menzies, for the
use of color for the enhancement of dramatic mood.

A stunning and haunting portrait of Vivien Leigh as Scarlett O'Hara.

Award winner Hattie McDaniel, and a great supporting cast of Barbara O'Neil, Alicia Rhett, and Thomas Mitchell.

GOODBYE, MR. CHIPS
M-G-M (British)

- **Best Actor:** Robert Donat

Portrait card of leads Greer Garson and Robert Donat.

STAGECOACH
Wanger, United Artists

- **Best Supporting Actor:** Thomas Mitchell
- **Music (Scoring):** Richard Hageman, Frank Harling, John Leipold, and Leo Shuken.

The old soldier next to Thomas Mitchell on the right is the only actor not credited on this wonderful and valuable lobby card. Left to right, we have: Donald Meek, John Wayne, Andy Devine, Claire Trevor, George Bancroft, Louise Platt, Tim Holt, John Carradine, Berton Churchill, old soldier, and Thomas Mitchell.

THE UGLY DUCKLING
Disney, RKO Radio

- **Short Subject:** Cartoon

With beauty being in the eye of the beholder, this different little duckling holds his own with the rest of the family.

BUSY LITTLE BEARS
Paramount

- **Short Subject (One-reel):** Paragraphics Series

SONS OF LIBERTY
Warner Brothers

- **Short Subject (Two-reel):** Historical Featurette

A serious moment in the creation of the Declaration of Independence.

THE WIZARD OF OZ
M-G-M

- **Music (Song):** "Over the Rainbow." Music by Harold Arlen. Lyrics by E.Y. Harburg.
- **Music (Original Score):** Herbert Stothart

The only lobby card that shows Jack Haley, Ray Bolger, Frank Morgan, Judy Garland, and Bert Lahr together. Here the Wizard prepares to depart at the end of the film.

WHEN TOMORROW COMES
Universal

- **Sound Recording:** Bernard B. Brown, Sound Director, Universal Studio Sound Dept.

It's an old story: love comes to a person who is already married to someone else! Irene Dunne and Charles Boyer are featured on this title card.

MR. SMITH GOES TO WASHINGTON
Columbia

- **Writing:** Lewis R. Foster

Portrait card of James Stewart and Jean Arthur.

WUTHERING HEIGHTS
Goldwyn, United Artists

- **Cinematography (Black-and-white):** Gregg Toland

Laurence Olivier as Heathcliff loves Merle Oberon in this romantic tragedy.

THE RAINS CAME
20th Century-Fox

- **Special Effects:** E.H. Hansen and Fred Sersen

Special effects saved this otherwise unspectacular drama, set in India. Tyrone Power (in turban), Myrna Loy, and George Brent are featured here.

1940

REBECCA
Selznick, United Artists

- **Best Picture:** produced by David O. Selznick
- **Cinematography (Black-and-white):** George Barnes

Laurence Olivier and Joan Fontaine are the stars, as is the famous house called Manderley.

THE PHILADELPHIA STORY
M-G-M

- **Best Actor:** James Stewart
- **Writing (Screenplay):** Donald Ogden Stewart

They need no introduction: Katharine Hepburn, Cary Grant, and James Stewart.

KITTY FOYLE
RKO Radio

- **Best Actress:** Ginger Rogers

Ginger Rogers plays the working girl, and this title card explains it all in the fine print.

THE WESTERNER
Goldwyn, United Artists

- **Best Supporting Actor:** Walter Brennan

Walter Brennan, Doris Davenport, and Gary Cooper all appear friendly, but Cooper and Brennan become deadly enemies in the final shoot-out.

THE GRAPES OF WRATH
20th Century-Fox

- **Best Supporting Actress:** Jane Darwell
- **Direction:** John Ford

Memorable Depression era film featuring (left to right): John Carradine, Doris Bowden, Henry Fonda, Jane Darwell, Russell Simpson, and Frank Darien.

THE THIEF OF BAGDAD
Korda, United Artists (British)

- **Special Effects:** Lawrence Butler and Jack Whitney
- **Cinematography (Color):** George Perinal
- **Art Direction (Color):** Vincent Korda

Sabu, June Duprez, and John Justin join forces to fight Conrad Veidt, the evil magician.

ARISE MY LOVE
Paramount

- **Writing (Original Story):** Benjamin Glazer and John S. Toldy

Ray Milland anticipates what Claudette Colbert has to say, as the pensive Miss Colbert writes notes for an article about War in Spain prior to World War II.

THE GREAT McGINTY
Paramount

- **Writing (Original Screenplay):** Preston Sturges

As Brian Donlevy (McGinty) is sworn in, Allyn Joslyn is seen left, and Muriel Angelus and William Demarest are at the right in this image.

NORTH WEST MOUNTED POLICE
DeMille, Paramount

- **Film Editing:** Anne Bauchens

Featured left to right are Gary Cooper, Madeleine Carroll, Preston Foster, Paulette Goddard, Robert Preston, and Lynne Overman.

STRIKE UP THE BAND
M-G-M

- **Sound Recording:** Douglas Shearer, Sound Director, M-G-M Studio Sound Dept.

Successfully paired in many musicals, Mickey Rooney and Judy Garland light up this lobby card.

PRIDE AND PREJUDICE
M-G-M

- **Art Direction:** Cedric Gibbons and Paul Groesse

PINOCCHIO
Disney, RKO Radio

- **Music (Song):** "When You Wish Upon a Star." Music by Leigh Harline, lyrics by Ned Washington.
- **Music (Original Score):** Leigh Harline, Paul J. Smith, and Ned Washington

Laurence Olivier and Greer Garson in an obviously romantic moment.

Gepetto creates Pinocchio while pets Cleo and Figaro smile approvingly.

Tin Pan Alley
20th Century-Fox

- **Music (Score):** Alfred Newman

Jack Oakie and John Payne (as songwriters in this film), show interest in Betty Grable and Alice Faye.

Milky Way
M-G-M

- **Short Subject (Cartoon):** Rudolph Ising Series

Quicker 'N a Wink
M-G-M

- **Short Subject (One-reel):** Pete Smith

Teddy, The Rough Rider
Warner Brothers

- **Short Subject (Two-reel):** Historic Featurette

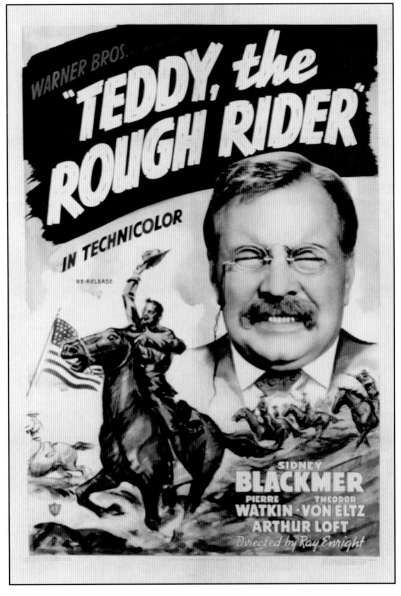

Sidney Blackmer looked the part in this title role.

1941

How Green Was My Valley
20th Century Fox

- **Best Picture:** Produced by Darryl F. Zanuck
- **Best Supporting Actor:** Donald Crisp
- **Direction:** John Ford
- **Cinematography (Black-and-white):** Arthur Miller
- **Art Direction-Interior Decoration:** Richard Day and Nathan Juran; Thomas Little

Almost all of the leading cast of this coal town drama are recognized here: Roddy McDowell, Maureen O'Hara, Donald Crisp, Patric Knowles, Sara Allgood, and John Loder.

Sergeant York
Warner Brothers

- **Best Actor:** Gary Cooper
- **Film Editing:** William Holmes

In this title role, Gary Cooper portrays a religious pacifist turned World War I hero, who captures a large group of German soldiers.

Suspicion
RKO Radio

- **Best Actress:** Joan Fontaine

Joan Fontaine certainly does not look suspicious of Cary Grant in this scene!

THE GREAT LIE
Warner Brothers

- **Best Supporting Actress:** Mary Astor

Mary Astor, George Brent, Hattie McDaniel, and Bette Davis star in this soap opera style movie.

ALL THAT MONEY CAN BUY
RKO Radio

- **Music (Scoring of a Dramatic Picture):** Bernard Herrmann.

In this film, Edward Arnold portrays Daniel Webster, whose soul is being hotly pursued by old Mr. Scratch, the devil. Interestingly enough, a title card such as this one tends to portray the lead stars, yet Mr. Arnold is not pictured. Shown are Simone Simon, Walter Huston, Anne Shirley, and James Craig.

LADY BE GOOD
M-G-M

- **Music (Song):** "The Last Time I Saw Paris." Music by Jerome Kern. Lyrics by Oscar Hammerstein II.

A great musical, and this card has it all. A dancing Eleanor Powell points to stars Ann Sothern and Robert Young, while small insets feature greats such as Red Skelton, John Carroll, and Lionel Barrymore.

DUMBO
Disney, RKO Radio

- **Music (Scoring of a Musical Picture):** Frank Churchill and Oliver Wallace

A great title card which shows all the characters in this animated classic.

Here Comes Mr. Jordan
Columbia

- **Writing (Original Story):** Harry Segall
- **Writing (Screenplay):** Sidney Buchman and Seton I. Miller

Mr. Jordan goes to heaven by accident in this comedy film. Shown on this title card, from left to right, are James Gleason, Edward Everett Horton, Rita Johnson, Robert Montgomery (as Mr. Jordan), Evelyn Keyes, and Claude Rains.

Citizen Kane
Mercury, RKO Radio

- **Writing (Original Screenplay):** Herman J. Mankiewicz and Orson Welles

Orson Welles, looking thin, stands tall in the top ten most famous film list.

I Wanted Wings
Paramount

- **Special Effects:** Farciot Edouart, Gordon Jennings, and Louis Mesenkop

Staring into the distance are, left to right, Ray Milland, Constance Moore, Harry Davenport, Brian Donlevy, Veronica Lake, and Wayne Morris.

Blood and Sand
20th Century Fox

- **Cinematography:** Ernest Palmer and Ray Rennahan

Rita Hayworth flirts with Anthony Quinn, and Tyrone Power appears not to appreciate the rapport between them.

Lend a Paw
Disney, RKO Radio

- **Short Subject:** Cartoon

Of Pups and Puzzles
M-G-M

- **Short Subject (One-reel):** Passing Parade Series

Main Street on the March
M-G-M

- **Short Subject (Two-reel):** Special

Blossoms in the Dust
M-G-M

- **Art Direction-Interior Decoration:** Cedric Gibbons and Urie McCleary; Edwin B. Willis

A happy moment between Walter Pidgeon and orphanage founder Greer Garson, in an otherwise often sad film.

That Hamilton Woman
Korda, United Artists

- **Sound Recording:** Jack Whitney, Sound Director, General Service Studio Sound Dept.

The romance between Vivien Leigh and Laurence Olivier happened in real life as well as in this film.

CHURCHILL'S ISLAND
Canadian Film Board, United Artists

- **Documentary**

KUKAN
United Artists

- **Special Award:** Rey Scott, producer, for 16 mm photography under extremely adverse conditions, while filming this chronicle of China's struggle.

Rey Scott is shown filming this United Artists historical piece.

TARGET FOR TONIGHT
Warner Brothers

- **Special Award:** To the British Ministry of Information , for the documenting of the heroism of the RAF.

This Warner Brothers documentary chronicles the war efforts of the British RAF.

FANTASIA
Disney, RKO Radio

- **Special Award:** Leopold Stokowski and his associates for their innovations in visualized music.
- **Special Award:** Walt Disney, William Garity, John N.A. Hawkins, and the RCA Manufacturing Company for their innovations in the use of sound in a motion picture, through their production of Fantasia.

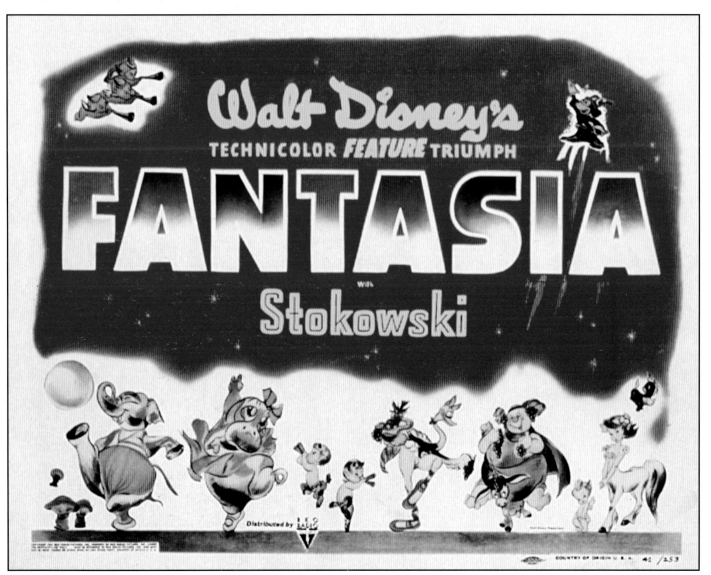

This creative film, a story in eight parts, features music throughout by Leopold Stokowski and the Philadelphia Orchestra. Mickey Mouse's "Sorcerer's Apprentice" is the most famous segment.

1942

MRS. MINIVER
M-G-M

- **Best Picture:** Produced by Sidney Franklin
- **Best Actress:** Greer Garson
- **Best Supporting Actress:** Teresa Wright
- **Direction:** William Wyler
- **Writing (Screenplay):** George Froeschel, James Hilton, Claudine West, and Arthur Wimperis
- **Cinematography:** Joseph Ruttenberg

"We must get back home!"

Greer Garson and Teresa Wright both won Academy Awards®, and gave the American public more reasons to support our English allies in World War II.

YANKEE DOODLE DANDY
Warner Brothers

- **Best Actor:** James Cagney
- **Sound Recording:** Nathan Levinson, Sound Director, Warner Bros. Studio Sound Dept.
- **Music (Scoring of a Musical Picture):** Ray Heindorf and Heinz Roemheld

Jeanne Cagney, James Cagney, and Joan Leslie sing and dance the title song. The story chronicles the life of George M. Cohan.

JOHNNY EAGER
M-G-M

- **Best Supporting Actor:** Van Heflin

Gangster Robert Taylor threatens Robert Sterling, while Van Heflin observes the exchange.

THE INVADERS
Ortus, Columbia (British)

- **Writing (Original Story):** Emeric Pressburger

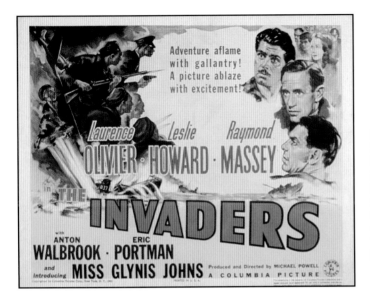

Laurence Olivier, Leslie Howard, and Raymond Massey star in this World War II adventure film about a Nazi U-boat which sank off the coast of Canada. The film was also titled "49th Parallel."

WOMAN OF THE YEAR
M-G-M

- **Writing (Original Screenplay):** Michael Kanin and Ring Lardner, Jr.

The chemistry was obvious between superstars Spencer Tracy and Katharine Hepburn in this film about two reporters who eventually married.

THE BLACK SWAN
20th Century Fox

- **Cinematography (Color):** Leon Shamroy

Tyrone Power grips the defiant Maureen O'Hara, as he protects her from pirate captain George Sanders.

THIS ABOVE ALL
20th Century Fox

- **Art Direction-Interior Decoration (Black-and-white):** Richard Day and Joseph Wright; Thomas Little

Tyrone Power (standing, center) finds love in England during World War II with Joan Fontaine. In this scene, they observe Thomas Mitchell (right) in a conversation.

My Gal Sal
20th Century Fox

- **Art Direction-Interior Decoration (Color):** Richard Day and Joseph Wright; Thomas Little

In this film, songwriter Victor Mature loves singer Rita Hayworth, who is featured three times on this card. Note that Phil Silvers is at the piano, with John Sutton nearby.

Reap the Wild Wind
DeMille, Paramount

- **Special Effects:** Farciot Edouart, Gordon Jennings, William L. Pereira, and Louis Mesenkop

Ray Milland, Paulette Goddard, John Wayne, and Susan Hayward star in an exciting underwater drama.

The Pride of the Yankees
Goldwyn, RKO

- **Film Editing:** Daniel Mandell

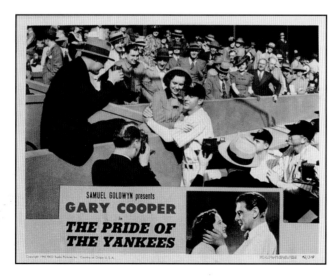

Co-stars Teresa Wright and Gary Cooper (as Lou Gehrig) are the pride of this film! Note Babe Ruth in uniform on the far right.

Der Fuehrer's Face
Disney, RKO Radio

- **Short Subject:** Cartoon

Donald throws a "Ve Heil right in Der Fuehrer's face!"

Speaking of Animals and Their Families
Paramount

- **Short Subject (One-reel)**

"In Winter Quarters" is the title on this stock sheet for the "Speaking of Animals" series.

Beyond the Line of Duty
Warner Brothers

- **Short Subject (Two-reel):** Broadway Brevities Series

Holiday Inn
Paramount

- **Music (Song):** "White Christmas." Music and lyrics by Irving Berlin

Bing Crosby, Virginia Dale, Fred Astaire, and Marjorie Reynolds sing and dance their way through the holidays of the calendar. The bestselling hit song "White Christmas," the snowy scenes, and the cozy ambiance of the Holiday Inn itself make this film a Christmas family favorite year after year.

Now, Voyager
Warner Brothers

- **Music (Scoring of a Dramatic or Comedy Picture):** Max Steiner

Paul Henreid, Bette Davis, and John Loder (left to right) in a story of a woman's emergence from shy spinsterhood.

Battle of Midway
U.S. Navy, 20ᵗʰ Century-Fox

- **Documentary**

The battle of Midway is considered by many to be the turning point of World War II against the Japanese.

Kokoda Front Line
Australian News Information Bureau

- **Documentary**

MOSCOW STRIKES BACK
Artkino (Russian)

- Documentary

Edward G. Robinson narrates this documentary about Russia's attack on Germany.

PRELUDE TO WAR
U.S. Army Special Services

- Documentary

Hirohito, Hitler, and Mussolini were enough to scare anyone as America prepared for war.

IN WHICH WE SERVE

- **Special Award:** Noel Coward for outstanding production achievement.

Noel Coward stars in this World War II naval historical classic.

1943

CASABLANCA
Warner Brothers

- **Best Picture**, produced by Hal B. Wallis
- **Direction:** Michael Curtiz
- **Writing (Screenplay):** Julius J. Epstein, Philip G. Epstein, and Howard Koch

Paul Henreid, Ingrid Bergman, Claude Rains, and Humphrey Bogart in the famous letter of transit scene in which Rick Blaine (Bogart) gets the letter for Victor Lazlo (Henreid) and shows his patriotic side.

WATCH ON THE RHINE
Warner Brothers

- **Best Actor:** Paul Lukas

Eric Roberts, Janis Wilson, Paul Lukas, Bette Davis, Donald Buka, and Donald Woods. The German underground fights fascism in this film.

THE SONG OF BERNADETTE
20th Century-Fox

- **Best Actress:** Jennifer Jones
- **Cinematography:** Arthur Miller
- **Art Direction-Interior Decoration (Black-and-white):** James Basevi and William Darling; Thomas Little
- **Music (Scoring of a Dramatic or Comedy Picture):** Alfred Newman

Alan Napier, Charles Bickford, Jennifer Jones, and Vincent Price star in this story of a visionary religious French girl (Jones).

FOR WHOM THE BELL TOLLS
Paramount

- **Best Supporting Actress:** Katina Paxinou

Katina Paxinou and Akim Tamiroff as Spanish Civil War mountain patriots in this Ernest Hemingway classic.

THE MORE THE MERRIER
Columbia

- **Best Supporting Actor:** Charles Coburn

Joel McCrea, Jean Arthur, and Charles Coburn share an apartment in this World War II comedy.

THE HUMAN COMEDY
M-G-M

- **Writing (Original Story):** William Saroyan

James Craig, Marsha Hunt, Frank Morgan, and Mickey Rooney star in this World War II story, set in small town USA

PRINCESS O'ROURKE
Warner Brothers

- **Writing (Original Screenplay):** Norman Krasna

Olivia de Havilland, Robert Cummings, Jane Wyman, and Jack Carson star in this light comedy.

THE PHANTOM OF THE OPERA
Universal

- **Cinematography (Color):** Hal Mohr and W. Howard Greene
- **Art Direction-Interior Decoration (Color):** Alexander Golitzen and John B. Goodman; Russell A. Gausman and Ira S. Webb

Claude Rains (Phantom) grabs Susanna Foster (soprano opera star), intending to take her to the catacombs in Paris.

THIS LAND IS MINE
RKO Radio

- **Sound Recording:** Stephen Dunn, Sound Director, RKO Radio Studio Sound Dept.

Spies and intrigue mark this World War II film. Here Walter Slezak examines the ring of Maureen O'Hara while a concerned George Sanders stands by.

AIR FORCE
Warner Brothers

- **Film Editing:** George Amy

John Garfield cradles a submachine gun and exchanges words with Gig Young, as bomber crews prepare to fight the Japanese on land.

CRASH DIVE
20th Century-Fox

- **Special Effects:** Fred Sersen and Roger Heman

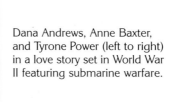

Dana Andrews, Anne Baxter, and Tyrone Power (left to right) in a love story set in World War II featuring submarine warfare.

HELLO FRISCO HELLO
20th Century-Fox

- **Music (Song):** "You'll Never Know." Music by Harry Warren. Lyrics by Mack Gordon.

Jack Oakie, Alice Faye, and John Payne together in yet another musical.

THIS IS THE ARMY
Warner Brothers

- **Music (Scoring of a Musical Picture):** Ray Heindorf

George Murphy, Ronald Reagan, Joan Leslie, and Charlie Butterworth star in this patriotic World War II musical.

YANKEE DOODLE MOUSE
M-G-M

- **Short Subject (Cartoon):** Fred Quimby, producer

AMPHIBIOUS FIGHTERS
Paramount

- **Short Subject (One-reel):** Grantland Rice, producer

HEAVENLY MUSIC
M-G-M

- **Short Subject (Two-reel):** Jerry Bresler and Sam Coslow, producers

Wonderful musical short with the stars pictured in caricature.

DECEMBER 7TH
U.S. Navy, Field Photographic Branch, Office of Strategic Services

- **Documentary (Short Subject)**

DESERT VICTORY
British Ministry of Information

- **Documentary (Feature)**

As this title card reads, this film is a feature about the rout of Rommel by the British Eighth Army.

1944

GOING MY WAY
Paramount

- **Best Picture:** Produced by Leo McCarey
- **Best Actor:** Bing Crosby
- **Best Supporting Actor:** Barry Fitzgerald
- **Direction:** Leo McCarey
- **Writing (Original Story):** Leo McCarey
- **Writing (Screenplay):** Frank Butler and Frank Cavett
- **Music:** "Swinging on a Star." Music by James Van Heusen. Lyrics by Johnny Burke.

Bing Crosby, Frank McHugh, and Barry Fitzgerald (left to right) sing their way to an award-winning film which tugs at the heart strings.

GASLIGHT
M-G-M

- **Best Actress:** Ingrid Bergman
- **Art Direction-Interior Decoration (Black-and-white):** Cedric Gibbons and William Ferrari; Edwin B. Willis and Paul Huldschinsky

Ingrid Bergman is being driven insane by her husband, Charles Boyer, while Joseph Cotton tries to help her.

NONE BUT THE LONELY HEART
RKO Radio

- **Best Supporting Actress:** Ethel Barrymore

Left to right: Cary Grant, Ethel Barrymore, Barry Fitzgerald, and Jane Wyatt star in this lighthearted crime film.

WILSON
20th Century-Fox

- **Writing (Original Screenplay):** Lamar Trotti
- **Cinematography (Color):** Leon Shamroy
- **Art Direction-Interior Decoration (Color):** Wiard Ihnen; Thomas Little
- **Film Editing:** Barbara McLean
- **Sound Recording:** E.H. Hansen, Sound Director, 20th Century-Fox Studio Sound Dept.

This title card heralds an historic film about President Woodrow Wilson. Clockwise, from the top, you see Charles Coburn, William Eythe, Mary Anderson, Geraldine Fitzgerald, Alexander Knox, and Thomas Mitchell.

LAURA
20th Century-Fox

- **Cinematography (Black-and-white):** Joseph LaShelle

Clifton Webb, Gene Tierney (Laura), Dana Andrews, Vincent Price, and Judith Anderson star in this popular film, whose theme was murder.

THIRTY SECONDS OVER TOKYO
M-G-M

- **Special Effects:** Arnold Gillespie, Donald Jahraus, Warren Newcombe, and Douglas Shearer

Phyllis Thaxter, Van Johnson (twice), Spencer Tracy, and Robert Walker star in an account of the famous Doolittle bombing raid of World War II.

Since You Went Away
Selznick, United Artists

- **Music (Scoring of a Dramatic or Comedy Picture):** Max Steiner

Cover Girl
Columbia

- **Music (Scoring of a Musical Picture):** Carmen Dragon and Morris Stoloff

From left to right: Claudette Colbert, Joseph Cotton, Jennifer Jones, Shirley Temple, Monty Woolley, Lionel Barrymore, and Robert Walker star in a poignant love story and World War II tragedy.

As the lobby card states, Rita Hayworth and Gene Kelly are brilliant in this musical film!

MOUSE TROUBLE
M-G-M

- **Short Subject (Cartoon):** Frederick C. Quimby, producer

WHO'S WHO IN ANIMAL LAND
Paramount

- **Short Subject (One-reel):** Speaking of Animals Series. Jerry Fairbanks, producer.

I WON'T PLAY
Warner Brothers

- **Short Subject (Two-reel):** Featurette. Gordon Hollingshead, producer.

WITH THE MARINES AT TARAWA
U.S. Marine Corps

- **Documentary (Short Subjects)**

THE FIGHTING LADY
20ᵗʰ Century-Fox and U.S. Navy

- **Documentary (Features)**

A true story of life on an aircraft carrier, photographed by the U.S. Navy.

Detailed artwork underscores the horror of the fighting chronicled by this documentary, an official Marine Corps film photographed by combat photographers and presented by the U.S. Government.

1945

THE LOST WEEKEND
Paramount

- **Best Picture:** Produced by Charles Brackett
- **Best Actor:** Ray Milland
- **Direction:** Billy Wilder
- **Writing (Screenplay):** Charles Brackett and Billy Wilder

Ray Milland struggles to conquer the disease of alcoholism as Jane Wyman and Phillip Terry show support.

MILDRED PIERCE
Warner Brothers

- **Best Actress:** Joan Crawford

Zachary Scott toasts Jack Carson and Joan Crawford.

A TREE GROWS IN BROOKLYN
20th Century-Fox

- **Best Supporting Actor:** James Dunn

James Dunn is surrounded by his family and friends in this title card from a film about the trials and tribulations of a family in Brooklyn.

NATIONAL VELVET
M-G-M

- **Best Supporting Actress:** Anne Revere
- **Film Editing:** Robert J. Kern

Clockwise: Jackie "Butch" Jenkins, Elizabeth Taylor, Donald Crisp, Anne Revere, and Mickey Rooney star in the film based on the famous novel of the same name.

THE HOUSE ON 92ND STREET
20th Century-Fox

- **Writing (Original Story):** Charles G. Booth

Lloyd Nolan, William Eythe (large image), Leo G. Carroll, Lydia St. Clair, and Signe Hasso are featured on this dramatic title card.

MARIE-LOUISE
Praesens Films (Swiss)

- **Writing (Original Screenplay):** Richard Schweizer

Josiane Hegg escapes to Switzerland from France to avoid Nazi cruelty in World War II.

THE PICTURE OF DORIAN GRAY
M-G-M

- **Cinematography:** Harry Stradling

Hurd Hatfield and Donna Reed have an uneasy love affair.

LEAVE HER TO HEAVEN
20th Century-Fox

- **Cinematography:** Leon Shamroy

Left to right: Cornel Wilde, Gene Tierney, Jeanne Crain, and Vincent Price in a love story that threatens death at every turn!

BLOOD ON THE SUN
Cagney, United Artists

- **Art Direction-Interior Decoration (Black-and-white):** Wiard Ihnen; A. Roland Fields

Set in prewar Japan, James Cagney finds himself fighting with both politicians and soldiers in this film! Sylvia Sidney looks just gorgeous on this portrait lobby card.

FRENCHMAN'S CREEK
Paramount

- **Art Direction-Interior Decoration (Color):** Hans Drier and Ernst Fegte; Sam Comer

Basil Rathbone chases Joan Fontaine in this historical adventure story.

THE BELLS OF ST. MARY'S
Rainbow, RKO Radio

- **Sound Recording:** Stephen Dunn, Sound Director, RKO Radio Sound Dept.

Bing Crosby and Ingrid Bergman star in this sequel to "Going My Way."

WONDER MAN
Goldwyn, RKO Radio

- **Special Effects:** John Fulton and A.W. Johns

Vera-Ellen, Danny Kaye, and Virginia Mayo star in this delightful musical comedy about twins…with a twist!

STATE FAIR
20th Century-Fox

- **Music (Song):** "It Might as Well be Spring." Music by Richard Rodgers. Lyrics by Oscar Hammerstein II.

Fay Bainter, Charles Winninger, Dana Andrews, Jeanne Crain, Dick Haymes, and Vivian Blaine star in a musical , set at the Iowa State Fair, that relates a family's adventures there.

SPELLBOUND
Selznick, United Artists

- **Music (Scoring of a Dramatic or Comedy Picture):** Miklos Rozsa

Ingrid Bergman and Gregory Peck star in this Alfred Hitchcock suspense classic.

ANCHORS AWEIGH
M-G-M

- **Music (Scoring of a Musical Picture):** Georgie Stoll

A fun musical which puts three young stars, Frank Sinatra, Kathryn Grayson, and Gene Kelly, together for the first and only time. One of the film's highlights involves tap dancing teamwork between Jerry (of Tom and Jerry cartoon fame!) and Gene Kelly, to create a fascinating combination of live dancing and animation.

QUIET PLEASE!
M-G-M

- **Short Subject (Cartoon):** Tom and Jerry Series, Frederick Quimby, producer

STAIRWAY TO LIGHT
M-G-M

- **Short Subject (One-reel):** (John Nesbitt Passing Parade), Herbert Moulton Producer

STAR IN THE NIGHT
Warner Brothers

- **Short Subject (Two-reel):** Broadway Brevities Series: Produced by Gordon Hollingshead

THE TRUE GLORY
Governments of Great Britain and U.S.A.

- **Documentary (Features)**

The real General Dwight D. Eisenhower and his servicemen.

THE HOUSE I LIVE IN
RKO Radio; produced by Frank Ross and Mervyn LeRoy; directed by Mervyn LeRoy; screenplay by Albert Maltz; music by Earl Robinson and Lewis Allen; starring Frank Sinatra.

- **Special Award:** Short Subject

This famous "short" stars Frank Sinatra. A poster from this film is on everyone's want list, but is impossible to find. Here Frank is inspiring a group of boys that include Ronnie Ralph.

1946

THE BEST YEARS OF OUR LIVES
Goldwyn, RKO Radio

- **Best Picture:** Produced by Samuel Goldwyn
- **Best Actor:** Fredric March
- **Best Supporting Actor:** Harold Russell
- **Direction:** William Wyler
- **Writing (Screenplay):** Robert E. Sherwood
- **Film Editing:** Daniel Mandell
- **Music (Scoring of a Dramatic or Comedy Picture):** Hugo Friedhofer
- **Special Award:** To Harold Russell, whose appearance in the film brought courage and hope to his fellow veterans.

Myrna Loy and Fredric March dance the night away as Best Supporting Actor Harold Russell looks on in his naval uniform

TO EACH HIS OWN
Paramount

- **Best Actress:** Olivia de Havilland

John Lund and Olivia de Havilland are about to kiss, but she doesn't seem too sure!

THE RAZOR'S EDGE
20th Century-Fox

- **Best Supporting Actress:** Anne Baxter

Left to right: Gene Tierney, Tyrone Power, Herbert Marshall, Clifton Webb, Anne Baxter, and Lucile Watson share this tragic tale of one woman's difficulties with love and alcoholism in Paris.

VACATION FROM MARRIAGE
London Films, M-G-M (British)

- **Writing (Original Story):** Clemence Dane

Robert Donat and Deborah Kerr star in this World War II love story.

THE SEVENTH VEIL
Rank, Universal (British)

- **Writing (Original Screenplay):** Muriel Box and Sydney Box

Herbert Lom, Ann Todd, and James Mason star in this psychotic thriller.

ANNA AND THE KING OF SIAM
20th Century-Fox

- **Cinematography (Black-and-white):** Arthur Miller
- **Art Direction-Interior Decoration (Black-and-white):** Lyle Wheeler and William Darling; Thomas Little and Frank E. Hughes

This title card is the only lobby card in the set of eight that shows the three principals: Linda Darnell, Irene Dunne, and Rex Harrison. This popular film was later remade as the musical, " The King and I."

The Yearling
M-G-M

- **Cinematography (Color):** Charles Rosher, Leonard Smith, and Arthur Arling
- **Art Direction-Interior Decoration (Color):** Cedric Gibbons and Paul Groesse; Edwin B. Willis

Claude Jarman Jr., Gregory Peck, and Jane Wyman star in this moving story about a boy and his deer.

The Jolson Story
Columbia

- **Sound Recording:** John Livadary, sound director, Columbia Studio Sound Dept.
- **Music (Scoring of a Musical Picture):** Morris Stoloff

Evelyn Keyes and Larry Parks grace this lobby card, despite the fact that a shot of Jolson doing the dance steps in "Swanee" would be a more appropriate image representing these awards!

Blithe Spirit
Rank-Two Cities, United Artists (British)

- **Special Effects:** Thomas Howard

Margaret Rutherford plays a medium who manages to bring back Rex Harrison's dead wife in a séance. She does such a good job that the dear departed one just refuses to go away, and instead stays on to haunt him in his new marriage. Left to right: Kay Hammond, Margaret Rutherford, and Rex Harrison.

THE HARVEY GIRLS
M-G-M

- **Music (Song):** "On the Atchison, Topeka, and the Santa Fe." Music by Harry Warren. Lyrics by Johnny Mercer.

Angela Lansbury, Judy Garland, and John Hodiak in a delightful musical set in the Old West.

THE CAT CONCERTO
M-G-M

- **Short Subject (Cartoon):** Tom and Jerry, Frederick Quimby, producer

FACING YOUR DANGER
Warner Brothers

- **Short Subject (One-reel):** Sports Parade - Gordon Hollingshead, producer

A BOY AND HIS DOG
Warner Brothers (Featurettes)

- **Short Subject (Two-reel): Featurettes** – Gordon Hollingshead, producer

Billy Sheffield and his dog protect each other.

SEEDS OF DESTINY
U.S. War Department

- **Documentary: Short Subject**

HENRY V
Rank-Two Cities, United Artists (British)

- **Special Award:** Laurence Olivier for outstanding achievement in producing, directing, and acting in *Henry V.*

Laurence Olivier and Renee Asherson star in this Shakespearean epic. This lobby card is a re-release.

GENTLEMAN'S AGREEMENT

20th Century-Fox

- **Best Picture:** Darryl F. Zanuck, Producer
- **Best Supporting Actress:** Celeste Holm
- **Direction:** Elia Kazan

Left to right: Gregory Peck, Celeste Holm, John Garfield, Gene Nelson, and Robert Karnes star in a film about prejudice.

A DOUBLE LIFE

Kanin, Universal - International

- **Best Actor:** Ronald Colman
- **Music (Scoring of a Dramatic or Comedy Picture):** Miklos Rozsa

Signe Hasso, Ronald Colman, and Shelley Winters are pictured on this title card for a theatrical murder mystery.

THE FARMER'S DAUGHTER

RKO Radio

- **Best Actress:** Loretta Young

A Swedish maid runs for Congress in this comedy featuring Joseph Cotton, Loretta Young, Charles Bickford, and Ethel Barrymore.

MIRACLE ON 34TH STREET
20th Century-Fox

- **Best Supporting Actor:** Edmund Gwenn
- **Writing (Original Story):** Valentine Davies
- **Writing (Screenplay):** George Seaton

Is he the real Santa Claus or isn't he? Edmund Gwenn as Kris Kringle, Maureen O'Hara, and John Payne discover the answer in this must-see holiday film, a perennial favorite.

THE BACHELOR AND THE BOBBY SOXER
RKO Radio

- **Writing (Original Screenplay):** Sidney Sheldon

Cary Grant, Shirley Temple, and Myrna Loy present a comedy in which Loy plays a judge who orders a bachelor (Grant) to date her sister (Temple) in an effort to quell the young girl's infatuation with him.

GREAT EXPECTATIONS
Rank Cineguild, Universal - International (British)

- **Cinematography (Black-and-white):** Guy Green
- **Art Direction-Set Decoration (Black-and-white):** John Bryan; Wilfred Singleton

Left to right: John Mills, Valerie Hobson, Jean Simmons, Anthony Wager, and Martita Hunt star in this Charles Dickens classic adventure.

BLACK NARCISSUS
Rank-Archer, Universal-International (British)

- **Cinematography (Color):** Jack Cardiff
- **Art Direction-Set Decoration (Color):** Alfred Junge

Sabu, Jean Simmons, Kathleen Byron, David Farrar, and Deborah Kerr are featured on this dramatically designed lobby card . A breathtaking Himalayan mission is the main setting for this film, which is gorgeous in both scenery and acting as well.

THE BISHOP'S WIFE
Goldwyn, RKO Radio

- **Sound Recording:** Gordon Sawyer, sound director, Samuel Goldwyn Studio Sound Dept.

Angel Cary Grant helps Bishop David Niven and his wife, Loretta Young, raise funds for a new church.

BODY AND SOUL
Enterprise, United Artists

- **Film Editing:** Francis Lyon and Robert Parrish

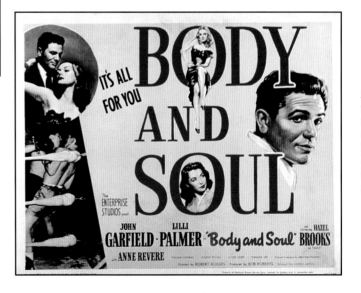

A boxing classic in which John Garfield uses every means, fair and otherwise, to become champion. Inserts in the title feature Hazel Brooks and Lili Palmer.

GREEN DOLPHIN STREET
M-G-M

- **Special Effects:** A. Arnold Gillespie, Warren Newcombe, Douglas Shearer, and Michael Steinore

SONG OF THE SOUTH
Disney, RKO Radio

- **Music (Song):** "Zip-A-Dee-Doo-Dah." Music by Allie Wrubel. Lyrics by Ray Gilbert.
- **Special Award:** James Baskett, for his warm and easy-going representation of Uncle Remus.

Lana Turner, Richard Hart, and Van Heflin star in this period piece about New Zealand.

This re-release lobby card shows Uncle Remus (James Baskett) surrounded by Brer Fox, Bobby Driscoll, Brer Bear, Luana Patten, and Brer Rabbit. A musical feast!

MOTHER WORE TIGHTS

20th Century-Fox

- **Music (Scoring of a Musical Picture):** Alfred Newman

Betty Grable and Dan Dailey strut their stuff in this pleasing musical.

TWEETIE PIE

Warner Brothers

- **Short Subject (Cartoon):** Merrie Melodies – Edward Selzer, producer

GOODBYE MISS TURLOCK

M-G-M

- **Short Subject (One-reel):** John Nesbitt Passing Parade Series – Herbert Moulton, producer

CLIMBING THE MATTERHORN

Monogram

- **Short Subjects (Two-reel):** Special – Irving Allen, Producer

Exciting short that leaves the viewer breathless.

FIRST STEPS

United Nations Division of Films and Visual Education

- **Documentary: Short Subject**

DESIGN FOR DEATH
RKO Radio

- **Documentary (Features):** Sid Rogell, Executive Producer; Theron Warth, and Richard O. Fleischer, Producers

An expose supported by secret Japanese film!

BILL AND COO
Republic

- **Special Award:** For the use of the medium of motion pictures in an innovating and entertaining way.

Ken Murray, Burton's Love Birds, Cannonball Twitchett, and Jimmy the Crow are the stars of this unique film!

SHOE-SHINE
Italy

- **Special Award:** For a triumphant, high quality of film-making under adverse conditions in a country recovering from the effects of war.

Pacifico Astrologo shines shoes while assisting with blackmarketing on the side.

HAMLET
Rank-Two Cities, Universal-International (British).

- **Best Picture:** Produced by Laurence Olivier
- **Best Actor:** Laurence Olivier
- **Art Direction-Set Decoration (Black-and-white):** Roger K. Furse; Carmen Dillon
- **Costume Design:** Roger K. Furse

JOHNNY BELINDA
Warner Brothers

- **Best Actress:** Jane Wyman

Lew Ayres and Jane Wyman star in this sympathetic story of a deaf-mute farm girl in Nova Scotia.

Basil Sydney, Eileen Herlie, and Laurence Olivier (Hamlet) consider what to do next.

THE TREASURE OF THE SIERRA MADRE
Warner Brothers

- **Best Supporting Actor:** Walter Huston
- **Direction:** John Huston
- **Writing (Screenplay):** John Huston

This classic story of lust for gold stars Walter Huston, Tim Holt, and Humphrey Bogart.

KEY LARGO
Warner Brothers

- **Best Supporting Actress:** Claire Trevor

Left to right: Claire Trevor, Lionel Barrymore, Humphrey Bogart, Edward G. Robinson, and Lauren Bacall star in this crime drama set in Florida during a tropical storm.

THE NAKED CITY
Hellinger, Universal-International

- **Cinematography (Black-and-white):** William Daniels
- **Film Editing:** Paul Weatherwax

Bottom to top: Don Taylor menaces Howard Duff, Dorothy Hart, and Barry Fitzgerald in this New York City crime drama.

JOAN OF ARC
Wanger-Sierra, RKO Radio

- **Cinematography (Color):** Joseph Valentine, William V. Skall, and Winton Hoch
- **Costume Design (Color):** Dorothy Jeakins and Madame Karinska
- **Special Award:** Walter Wanger for producing this film and thereby elevating the stature of the motion picture industry in the world.

This title lobby card portrays Joan of Arc's history as the savior of France. Ingrid Bergman, at left, majestically poses in her title role.

THE SEARCH
M-G-M (Swiss)

- **Writing (Motion Picture Story):** Richard Schweizer and David Wechsler
- **Special Award:** Ivan Jandl for his outstanding performance (juvenile) in the year 1948.

THE RED SHOES
Rank-Archers, Eagle-Lion (British)

- **Art Direction-Set Decoration (Color):** Hein Heckroth, Arthur Lawson
- **Music (Scoring of a Dramatic or Comedy Picture):** Brian Easdale

The fusion of dance and storytelling makes this the perfect movie for ballet lovers. Moira Shearer and Robert Helpmann star.

Montgomery Clift, Wendell Corey, and Aline MacMahon in a story of postwar Berlin. Clift looks after a concentration camp survivor, while his mother searches tirelessly for him at the same time.

THE SNAKE PIT
20th Century-Fox

- **Sound Recording:** 20th Century-Fox Sound Department

Olivia de Havilland, Mark Stevens (center), and Leo Genn (lower right corner) star in a film about mental illness, recovery, and the institutional life of patients

Portrait of Jennie
Selznick Releasing Organization

- **Special Effects:** Paul Eagler, J. McMillan Johnson, Russell Shearman, Clarence Slifer, Charles Freeman, and James G. Stewart.

Jennifer Jones and Joseph Cotton share love that was not meant to be.

The Little Orphan
M-G-M

- **Short Subject (Cartoon):** Tom and Jerry. Fred Quimby, producer.

Symphony of a City
20ᵗʰ Century- Fox

- **Short Subject (One-reel):** Movietone Specialty – Edmund R. Reek, producer.

Seal Island
Disney, RKO Radio

- **Short Subject (Two-reel):** True-life Adventure. Walt Disney, producer.

Seals are the stars of this enjoyable short!

Toward Independence
U.S. Army

- **Documentary (Short Subject)**

THE SECRET LAND
U.S. Navy, M-G-M

- **Documentary (Short Subject):**
  O.O. Dull, producer

Robert Montgomery, Robert Taylor, and Van Heflin narrate this documentary tracing Admiral Byrd's mission to the Antarctic.

EASTER PARADE
M-G-M

- **Music (Scoring of a Musical Picture):** Johnny Green and Roger Edens

Judy Garland and Fred Astaire nearly dance their way right off this lobby card!

THE PALEFACE
Paramount

- **Music (Song):** "Buttons and Bows." Music and lyrics by Jay Livingstone and Ray Evans.

A western and a comedy at the same time, this film is a parody of "The Virginian." Jane Russell (as Calamity Jane) and Bob Hope star.

MONSIEUR VINCENT
French

- **Special Award:** Most Outstanding Foreign Film released in the United States in 1948.

The biography of St. Vincent de Paul stars Pierre Fresnay as Monsieur Vincent.

1949

ALL THE KING'S MEN
Rossen, Columbia

- **Best Picture:** Produced by Robert Rossen
- **Best Actor:** Broderick Crawford

ALL THE KING'S MEN
Rossen, Columbia

- **Best Supporting Actress:** Mercedes McCambridge

Broderick Crawford has a few choice words for the slumped John Derek, while Anne Seymour looks on, and John Ireland holds back an angry political supporter.

Best Supporting Actress Mercedes McCambridge in her first film. She is featured on this lobby card only, shown here with John Ireland.

THE HEIRESS
Paramount

- **Best Actress:** Olivia de Havilland
- **Art Direction-Set Decoration (Black-and-white):** John Meehan and Harry Horner; Emile Kuri
- **Music (Scoring of a Dramatic or Comedy Picture):** Aaron Copland
- **Costume Design (Black-and-white):** Edith Head and Gile Steele

12 O'CLOCK HIGH
20th Century-Fox

- **Best Supporting Actor:** Dean Jagger
- **Sound Recording:** Fox Sound Department

Left to right: Clifton Webb, Olivia de Havilland, and Ralph Richardson. Clifton woos Olivia, but father Ralph suspects a fortune hunter.

Left to right: Gary Merrill, Gregory Peck, and Dean Jagger debate Air Force policy. Peck wins!

A Letter to Three Wives
20th Century-Fox

- **Direction:** Joseph L. Mankiewicz
- **Writing (Screenplay):** Joseph L. Mankiewicz

Left to right: Jeanne Crain, Linda Darnell, and Ann Sothern are married to Jeffrey Lynn, Paul Douglas, and Kirk Douglas…but one of them has gone off with another woman and the three wives don't know which husband has strayed.

Little Women
M-G-M

- **Art Direction-Set Decoration (Color):** Cedric Gibbons and Paul Groesse; Edwin B. Willis and Jack D. Moore

Margaret O'Brien, Janet Leigh, Elizabeth Taylor, June Allyson, and Peter Lawford star in this famous remake.

The Stratton Story
M-G-M

- **Writing (Motion Picture Story):** Douglas Morrow

"We're stepping out tonight!"

June Allyson, Agnes Moorehead, and James Stewart as Monty Stratton star in a success story about a one-legged baseball player.

BATTLEGROUND
M-G-M

- **Cinematography (Black-and-white):** Paul C. Vogel
- **Writing (Story and Screenplay):** Robert Pirosh

A scene from the realistic war drama about the Battle of the Bulge.

SHE WORE A YELLOW RIBBON
Argosy- RKO Radio

- **Cinematography (Color):** Winton Hoch

This John Ford directed classic western stars John Wayne, Joanne Dru, John Agar, and Harry Carey, Jr.. Ben Johnson is pictured at lower right.

CHAMPION
Kramer, United Artists

- **Film Editing:** Harry Gerstad

Kirk Douglas boxes and loves his way to the top, leaving fighters and women in his wake. The ladies are (left to right) Ruth Roman, Lola Albright, and Marilyn Maxwell.

MIGHTY JOE YOUNG
Cooper, RKO Radio

• **Special Effects**

This artistic title card shows Mighty Joe Young (the ape) saving a little girl. That's Ben Johnson climbing the rope, and Terry Moore being lifted while playing the piano.

NEPTUNE'S DAUGHTER
M-G-M

• **Music:** "Baby its Cold Outside." Music and lyrics by Frank Loesser.

ON THE TOWN
M-G-M

• **Music (Scoring of a Musical Picture):** Roger Edens and Lennie Hayton

Left to right: Frank Sinatra, Betty Garrett, Jules Munshin, Ann Miller, Gene Kelly, and Vera-Ellen star in this New York City musical.

Ricardo Montalban is seen romancing Esther Williams, yet she bestows an aquatic kiss upon funny man Red Skelton in this swimmingly funny musical.

For Scent-imental Reasons
Warner Brothers

- **Short Subject (Cartoon):** Looney Tunes, Edward Selzer, producer

Aquatic House Party
Paramount

- **Short Subject (One-reel):** Grantland Rice Sportlights – Jack Eaton, producer

Van Gogh
Canton-Weiner

- **Short Subject (Two-reel):** Gaston Diehl and Robert Haessans, producers

Adventures of Don Juan
Warner Brothers

- **Costume Design (Color):** Leah Rhodes, Travilla and Marjorie Best

A Chance to Live
March of Time, 20th Century-Fox

- **Documentary (Short Subject):** Richard deRochemont, producer

So Much for So Little
Warner Brothers

- **Documentary (Short Subject):** Edward Selzer, producer

Daybreak in Udi
British Informational Services

- **Documentary (Feature):** Crown Film Unit, producer

The Bicycle Thief
Italian

- **Special Award:** Most outstanding foreign language film released in the United States in 1949

Viveca Lindfors sends an admiring glance toward swordsman Errol Flynn.

A father and son interact in a story of their life and how it changes when the bicycle that is essential to their livelihood is stolen.

1950

ALL ABOUT EVE
20th Century-Fox

- **Best Picture:** Produced by Darryl F. Zanuck
- **Best Supporting Actor:** George Sanders
- **Direction:** Joseph L. Mankiewicz
- **Writing (Screenplay):** Joseph L. Mankiewicz
- **Costume Design (Black-and-white):** Edith Head and Charles LeMaire
- **Sound Recording:** 20th Century-Fox Sound Department

CYRANO DE BERGERAC
Kramer, United Artists

- **Best Actor:** Jose Ferrer

Was there ever a better Cyrano than Jose Ferrer? As this title card says, "Fabulous hero! Famous nose!"

BORN YESTERDAY
Columbia

- **Best Actress:** Judy Holliday

Gary Merrill (who married Bette Davis in real life), watches diva Bette apprehensively as she congratulates crafty Anne Baxter. George Sanders appreciates the moment.

This 1961 re-release lobby card shows all three of the leads in this amusing comedy. William Holden coaches Judy Holliday on how to be more sophisticated, while her boyfriend Broderick Crawford encourages her.

HARVEY

Universal - International

- **Best Supporting Actress:** Josephine Hull

Victoria Horne, Jesse White, Josephine Hull, Cecil Kellaway, Wallace Ford , James Stewart, and Harvey the Rabbit star in this entertaining comedy.

PANIC IN THE STREETS

20th Century-Fox

- **Writing (Motion Picture Story):** Edna Anhalt and Edward Anhalt

Barbara Bel Geddes and Richard Widmark star in a gangster story set in New Orleans.

SUNSET BOULEVARD

Paramount

- **Writing (Story and Screenplay):** Charles Brackett, Billy Wilder, and D.M. Marshman Jr.
- **Art Direction-Set Decoration (Black-and-white):** Hans Drier and John Meehan; Sam Comer and Ray Moyer
- **Music (Scoring of a Dramatic or Comedy Picture):** Franz Waxman

Left to right: William Holden, Gloria Swanson, and Eric von Stroheim in a classic story of a silent actress's attempt to reclaim stardom.

THE THIRD MAN
Selznick-London Films, SRO (British)

- **Cinematography (Black-and-white):** Robert Krasker

Valli, Joseph Cotton, and Trevor Howard search for Harry Lime (played by Orson Welles) in Vienna.

KING SOLOMON'S MINES
M-G-M

- **Cinematography (Color):** Robert Surtees
- **Film Editing:** Ralph E. Winters and Conrad A. Nervig

Stewart Granger, a native guide, Deborah Kerr, and Richard Carlson search for the lost mines of King Solomon.

SAMSON AND DELILAH
DeMille, Paramount

- **Art Direction-Set Decoration (Color):** Hans Dreier and Walter Tyler; Sam Comer and Ray Moyer
- **Costume Design (Color):** Edith Head, Dorothy Jeakins, Elois Jenssen, Gile Steele, and Gwen Wakeling

Hedy Lamarr and Angela Lansbury compete for attention from lion killer Victor Mature.

DESTINATION MOON
Pal, Eagle Lion

- **Special Effects**

This lobby card is from one of the first 1950s science fiction movies.

CAPTAIN CAREY, U.S.A.
Paramount

- **Music (Song):** "Mona Lisa." Music and lyrics by Ray Evans and Jay Livingston.

Alan Ladd and Wanda Hendrix star in this post World War II film set in Italy. They seek to find an informer who betrayed local villagers.

ANNIE GET YOUR GUN
M-G-M

- **Music (Scoring of a Musical Picture):** Adolph Deutsch and Roger Edens

Betty Hutton beats Howard Keel in a shooting match. Louis Calhern congratulates, her while Keenan Wynn holds her winnings.

GERALD McBOING-BOING
UPA, Columbia

- **Short Subject (Cartoons):** Jolly Frolics Series – Stephen Bosustow, Executive Producer.

Gerald tries to catch the freight train!

GRANDAD OF RACES
Warner Brothers

- **Short Subject:** Sports Parade Series – Gordon Hollingshead, producer

IN BEAVER VALLEY
Disney, RKO Radio

- **Short Subject (Two-reel; True-Life Adventure):** Walt Disney, Producer.

This colorful one-sheet shows all the problems in the life of a beaver.

WHY KOREA?
20th Century-Fox Movietone

- **Documentary (Short Subject):** Edmund Reek, producer

THE TITAN: STORY OF MICHELANGELO
Michelangelo Co., Classics Pictures, Inc.

- **Documentary (Feature):** Robert Snyder, Producer

Famous statue observed by the students of Michelangelo.

THE WALLS OF MALAPAGA
Franco-Italian

- **Honorary Award:** For the best foreign language film released in the United States in 1950.

Jean Gabin and Isa Miranda are the stars of this gripping drama.

AN AMERICAN IN PARIS
M-G-M

- **Best Picture:** Produced by Robert Freed
- **Writing (Story and Screenplay):** Alan Jay Lerner
- **Cinematography (Color):** Alfred Gilks and John Alton
- **Art Direction-Set Decoration (Color):** Cedric Gibbons and Preston Ames; Edwin B. Willis and Keogh Gleason
- **Music (Scoring of a Musical Picture):** Johnny Green and Saul Chaplin
- **Costume Design (Color):** Orry-Kelly, Walter Plunkett and Irene Sharaff

THE AFRICAN QUEEN
Horizon, United Artists

- **Best Actor:** Humphrey Bogart

Katharine Hepburn is impressed by Humphrey Bogart's skill at conning the Germans.

This musical bonanza, none of which was filmed in Paris, has it all! Vincente Minnelli directed a classic indeed. Gene Kelly, Leslie Caron, Oscar Levant, and Georges Guetary are the musical stars.

A Streetcar Named Desire
Charles K. Feldman, Warner Brothers

- **Best Actress:** Vivien Leigh
- **Best Supporting Actor:** Karl Malden
- **Best Supporting Actress:** Kim Hunter
- **Art Direction-Set Decoration (Black-and-white):** Richard Day; George James Hopkins

A Place in the Sun
Paramount

- **Direction:** George Stevens
- **Writing (Screenplay):** Michael Wilson and Harry Brown
- **Music (Scoring of a Dramatic or Comedy Picture):** Franz Waxman
- **Cinematography (Black-and-white):** William C. Mellor
- **Costume Design (Black-and-white):** Edith Head
- **Film Editing:** William Hornbeck

Kim Hunter, Marlon Brando, and Vivien Leigh are seen at odds in this re-release lobby card.

Elizabeth Taylor succumbs to the charms of Montgomery Clift.

Seven Days to Noon
Boulting Brothers, Mayer-Kingsley (British)

- **Writing (Motion Picture Story):** Paul Dehn and James Bernard

Barry Jones stars in this British film short about a scientist who threatens to blow up buildings in London.

Two Mouseketeers
M-G-M

- **Short Subject (Cartoon):** Tom and Jerry – Fred Quimby, producer

World of Kids
Warner Brothers

- **Short Subject (One-reel):** Vitaphone Novelties – Robert Youngson, producer

Nature's Half Acre
Disney, RKO Radio

- **Short Subject (Two-reel):** True-Life Adventure – Walt Disney, Producer

Strangely enough, this lobby card promoting a Technicolor film is printed in brown and white!

Benjy
Paramount Pictures Corp.

- **Documentary (Short Subject):** Fred Zinnemann for the Los Angeles Orthopaedic Hospital

Kon-Tiki
Artfilm Production, RKO Radio (Norwegian)

- **Documentary:** Olle Nordemar, Producer

Thor Heyerdahl and his raft sail from Peru to Tahiti.

When Worlds Collide
Pal, Paramount

- **Special Effects**

Barbara Rush and Richard Derr are threatened by a collision with another planet.

Here Comes the Groom
Paramount

- **Music (Song):** "In the Cool, Cool, Cool of the Evening." Music by Hoagy Carmichael. Lyrics by Johnny Mercer.

Bing Crosby and Cass Daley entertain the band while Frank Fontaine (Crazy Guggenheim) makes his famous face.

THE GREAT CARUSO
M-G-M

- **Sound Recording:** Douglas Shearer, sound director

RASHO-MON
Japanese

- **Honorary Award:** Most outstanding foreign language film released in the United States during 1951

Mario Lanza and Ann Blyth share song and fame in this musical biography of Enrico Caruso.

Toshiro Mifune and Machiko Kyo star in this Japanese classic about truth and human nature.

1952

THE GREATEST SHOW ON EARTH
DeMille, Paramount

- **Best Picture:** Produced by Cecil B. DeMille.
- **Writing (Motion Picture Story):** Frederick M. Frank, Theodore St. John, and Frank Cavett

Left to right: Charlton Heston, Betty Hutton, and Cornel Wilde star in this tale of circus life.

HIGH NOON
Kramer, United Artists

- **Best Actor:** Gary Cooper
- **Film Editing:** Elmo Williams and Harry Gerstad
- **Music (Song):** "High Noon (Do Not Forsake Me, Oh My Darlin')." Music by Dimitri Tiomkin. Lyrics by Ned Washington.
- **Music (Scoring of a Dramatic or Comedy Picture):** Dimitri Tiomkin

Gary Cooper dominates this title card, just as he dominates this film. Note glimpses of Grace Kelly, who portrays his wife, in the bottom two inserts.

COME BACK LITTLE SHEBA
Wallis, Paramount

- **Best Actress:** Shirley Booth

Left to right: Burt Lancaster, Shirley Booth, Terry Moore, and Richard Jaeckel star in this tale of affection gained and lost.

VIVA ZAPATA!
20th Century-Fox

- **Best Supporting Actor:** Anthony Quinn

Anthony Quinn and Marlon Brando star in the heroic tale of the Mexican Revolution against Spain.

THE BAD AND THE BEAUTIFUL
M-G-M

- **Best Supporting Actress:** Gloria Grahame
- **Writing (Screenplay):** Charles Schnee
- **Cinematography (Black-and-white):** Robert Surtees
- **Art Direction-Set Decoration (Black-and-white):** Cedric Gibbons and Edward Carfagno; Edwin B. Willis and Keogh Gleason
- **Costume Design (Black-and-white):** Helen Rose

Gloria Grahame won her award at the peak of her career. Here this southern belle, playing her usually provocative role, is married to Dick Powell.

THE QUIET MAN
Argosy, Republic

- **Direction:** John Ford
- **Cinematography (Color):** Winton C. Hoch and Archie Stout

Maureen O'Hara receives flowers from John Wayne while her difficult brother, Victor McLaglen, glowers.

THE LAVENDER HILL MOB
Rank-Ealing, Universal - International (British)

- **Writing (Story and Screenplay):** T.E.B. Clarke

Alec Guinness (left), a shy bank clerk, plans the perfect robbery with the help of Stanley Holloway. A wonderful comedy!

MOULIN ROUGE
Romulus, United Artists

- **Art Direction-Set Decoration (Color):** Paul Sheriff; Marcel Vertes
- **Costume Design (Color):** Marcel Vertes

Zsa Zsa Gabor and Jose Ferrer star in the story of French painter Toulouse Lautrec.

PLYMOUTH ADVENTURE
M-G-M

- **Special Effects**

Spencer Tracy and Gene Tierney are voyagers on the "Mayflower," sailing for New England in the 17th century.

BREAKING THE SOUND BARRIER
London Films, United Artists (British)

- **Sound Recording:** London Film Sound Department

Nigel Patrick and Ann Todd look to heaven as they are about to break the sound barrier.

WITH A SONG IN MY HEART
20th Century-Fox

- **Music (Scoring of a Musical Picture):** Alfred Newman

Susan Hayward (as Jane Froman) sings for the troops in this biographical film.

JOHANN MOUSE
M-G-M

- **Short Subject (Cartoon):** Tom and Jerry, Fred Quimby, producer

LIGHT IN THE WINDOW
Art Films Productions, 20th Century-Fox

- **Short Subject (One-reel):** Art Series – Boris Vermont, producer

WATER BIRDS
Disney, RKO Radio

- **Short Subject (Two-reel):** Time-Life Adventure – Walt Disney, Producer

This lobby card makes the movie's theme pretty clear!

NEIGHBOURS
Naional Film Board of Canada, Mayer-Kingsley, Inc. (Canadian)

- **Short Subject:** Norman McLaren, producer

THE SEA AROUND US
RKO Radio

- **Documentary (Feature):** Irwin Allen, Producer

A documentary by Rachel Carson about the marvels of life under water.

FORBIDDEN GAMES
French

- **Honorary Award:** Best Foreign Language Film released in the United States in 1952

George Poujouly and Brigitte Fossey play their games. The guitar theme is absolutely haunting.

1953

FROM HERE TO ETERNITY
Columbia

- **Best Picture:** Produced by Buddy Adler
- **Best Supporting Actor:** Frank Sinatra
- **Best Supporting Actress:** Donna Reed
- **Direction:** Fred Zinneman
- **Writing (Screenplay):** Daniel Taradash
- **Cinematography (Black-and-white):** Burnett Guffey
- **Sound Recording:** John P. Livadary, sound director, Columbia Sound Dept.
- **Film Editing:** William Lyon

The Academy Award™ winners Frank Sinatra (as Maggio) and Donna Reed seek friendship in a Hawaiian social club before the Pearl Harbor attack.

STALAG 17
Paramount

- **Best Actor:** William Holden

Left to right: Neville Brand, Don Taylor, William Holden, Robert Strauss, Harvey Lembeck, Michael Moore, Jay Lawrence, Peter Graves, and Richard Erdman star in the World War II story of a German prison camp.

ROMAN HOLIDAY
Paramount

- **Best Actress:** Audrey Hepburn
- **Writing (Motion Picture Story):** Dalton Trumbo
- **Costume Design (Black-and-white):** Edith Head

Photographer Eddie Albert captures the romance of journalist Gregory Peck and Princess Audrey Hepburn in the film that made Hepburn a star.

TITANIC
20th Century-Fox

- **Writing (Story and Screenplay):** Charles Brackett, Walter Reisch, and Richard Breen

Audrey Dalton, Barbara Stanwyck, Harper Carter, and Clifton Webb vie for lifeboat positions as the Titanic sinks.

SHANE
Paramount

- **Cinematography (Color):** Loyal Griggs

JULIUS CAESAR
M-G-M

- **Art Direction-Set Decoration (Black-and-white):** Cedric Gibbons and Edward Carfagno; Edwin B. Willis and Hugh Hunt

Left to right: Louis Calhern, Deborah Kerr, James Mason, Marlon Brando (as Caesar), Greer Garson, Mason again, John Gielgud, and Edmund O'Brien in the sterling cast for this epic of Rome and all its power.

Alan Ladd as Shane, Jean Arthur, and Van Heflin keep outlaws at bay.

THE ROBE
20th Century-Fox

- **Art Direction-Set Decoration (Color):** Lyle Wheeler and George W. Davis; Walter M. Scott and Paul S. Fox
- **Costume Design (Color):** Charles LeMaire and Emile Santiago

Jean Simmons receives the robe from Richard Burton, while the emperor, Jay Robinson, glares.

THE WAR OF THE WORLDS
Pal, Paramount

- **Special Effects**

This re-release card, showing the space ships attacking earth, did not appear in the original set of eight. At lower right, Gene Barry and Ann Robinson cower in fear.

CALAMITY JANE
Warner Brothers

- **Music (Song):** "Secret Love." Music by Sammy Fain. Lyrics by Paul Francis Webster.

Howard Keel (Wild Bill Hickok) sings to Doris Day (Calamity Jane) in this fun musical.

Lili

M-G-M

- **Music (Scoring of a Dramatic or Comedy Picture):** Bronislau Kaper

Orphan Leslie Caron hugs Mel Ferrer, who plays the puppeteer in this charming musical.

Call Me Madam

20th Century-Fox

- **Music (Scoring of a Musical Picture):** Alfred Newman

Left to right: Donald O'Connor, Ethel Merman, George Sanders, and Vera-Ellen star in this musical.

Toot, Whistle, Plunk, and Boom

Disney, Buena Vista

- **Short Subject (Cartoon):** Special Music Series - Walt Disney, producer

The Merry Wives of Windsor Overture

M-G-M

- **Short Subject (One-reel):** Overture Series – Johnny Green, producer

Bear Country

Disney, RKO Radio

- **Short Subject (Two-reel):** True-Life Adventure – Walt Disney, Producer

The highlight of this film is when the bears rub themselves against the trees in time to music!

THE ALASKAN ESKIMO
Disney, RKO Radio

- **Documentary (Short Subject):** Walt Disney, Producer

This studio won four Oscars™ in 1953.

THE LIVING DESERT
Disney, Buena Vista

- **Documentary (Feature):**
  Walt Disney, Producer

A not-so typical scene in the desert!

PETE SMITH SPECIALTIES
M-G-M

- **Honorary Award:** To Pete Smith for his clever comments and observations on American life.

This film is an example of Pete Smith specialty comedy.

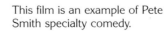

1954

On the Waterfront
Columbia, Horizon-American

- **Best Picture:** Produced by Sam Spiegel
- **Best Actor:** Marlon Brando
- **Best Supporting Actress:** Eve Marie Saint
- **Direction:** Elia Kazan
- **Writing (Story and Screenplay):** Budd Schulberg
- **Cinematography (Black-and-white):** Boris Kaufman
- **Film Editing:** Gene Milford
- **Art Direction-Set Decoration (Black-and-White):** Richard Day

Karl Malden and Eva Marie Saint tend to a beaten Marlon Brando.

The Country Girl
Perlberg-Seaton, Paramount

- **Best Actress:** Grace Kelly
- **Writing (Screenplay):** George Seaton

William Holden is fed up with Grace Kelly's support of alcoholic Bing Crosby.

The Barefoot Contessa
Figaro, United Artists

- **Best Supporting Actor:** Edmond O'Brien

Sultry Spanish dancer Ava Gardner is shown just having performed for Warren Stevens (left), Edmond O'Brien (right), and Humphrey Bogart (standing).

BROKEN LANCE
20th Century-Fox

- **Writing (Motion Picture Story):** Philip Yordan

Left to right: Spencer Tracy, Robert Wagner, Jean Peters, Richard Widmark, and Hugh O'Brien (insert, lower right).

20,000 LEAGUES UNDER THE SEA
Disney, Buena Vista

- **Art Direction-Set Decoration (Color):** John Meehan, Emile Kuri
- **Special Effects:** Walt Disney Studios

James Mason as Captain Nemo toasts Kirk Douglas, Peter Lorre, and Paul Lukas aboard the Nautilus in this classic Jules Verne story.

THREE COINS IN THE FOUNTAIN
20th Century-Fox

- **Cinematography (Color):** Milton Krasner
- **Music (Song):** "Three Coins in the Fountain." Music by Jule Styne. Lyrics by Sammy Cahn.

Left to right: Clifton Webb, Dorothy McGuire, Louis Jourdan, Maggie McNamara, Rossano Brazzi, and Jean Peters try to fulfill the wishes of the three girls who threw coins over their shoulders at the Trevi Fountain in Rome, looking for love.

SABRINA
Paramount

- **Costume Design (Black-and-white):** Edith Head

This re-release 1962 lobby card shows William Holden flirting with Audrey Hepburn (Sabrina), not realizing that she is the now grown-up chauffeur's daughter returned from Paris. Older brother Humphrey Bogart (far left) winds up being the lucky winner of Sabrina's affection.

GATE OF HELL
Daiei, Edward Harrison (Japanese)

- **Costume Design (Color):** Sanzo Wada
- **Honorary Award:** Best foreign language film released in the United States during 1954

This is the one-sheet for an exciting Japanese 12th century historical Samurai classic.

THE HIGH AND THE MIGHTY
Wayne Fellows, Warner Brothers

- **Music (Scoring of a Dramatic or Comedy Picture):** Dimitri Tiomkin

Left to right: passengers Jan Sterling, David Brian, Claire Trevor, John Wayne, John Smith, and Karen Sharpe share a scary airplane adventure.

THE GLENN MILLER STORY
Universal International

- **Sound Recording:** Leslie I. Carey, sound director

June Allyson and James Stewart star in this wonderful biography of big band leader and musician Glenn Miller.

SEVEN BRIDES FOR SEVEN BROTHERS
M-G-M

- **Music (Scoring of a Musical Picture):** Adolph Deutsch and Saul Chaplin

Jane Powell, wife of Howard Keel, tries to handle Keel and his brothers living up in the mountains, as they prepare to hunt for brides in the valley below (note Russ Tamblyn on far right).

THE VANISHING PRAIRIE
Disney, Buena Vista

- **Documentary (Feature):** Walt Disney, Producer

This documentary portrays the fate of the prairie and its bison.

WHEN MAGOO FLEW
UPA, Columbia

- **Short Subject (Cartoon):** Stephen Bosustow, producer

THIS MECHANICAL AGE
Warner Brothers

- **Short Subject (One-reel):** Robert Youngson, producer

A TIME OUT OF WAR
Carnival Productions

- **Short Subject (Two-reel):** Denis and Terry Sanders, producers

THURSDAY'S CHILDREN
British Information Services (British)

- **Documentary (Short Subject):** World Wide Pictures and Morse Films, producers

THE LITTLE KIDNAPPERS
British

- **Honorary Award:** Jon Whiteley for his outstanding juvenile performance
- **Honorary Award:** Vincent Winter for his outstanding performance

This title card features the four major stars of the film: Vincent Winter, Jon Whitely, Adrienne Corri, and Duncan MacRae.

TO CATCH A THIEF
Hitchcock, Paramount

- **Cinematography (Color):** Robert Burks

Two cool and beautiful people, Cary Grant and Grace Kelly, romance in this gripping crime story.

PICNIC
Columbia

- **Art Direction-Set Decoration (Color):** William Flannery and Jo Mielziner; Robert Priestley
- **Film Editing:** Charles Nelson and William A. Lyon

Kim Novak and Susan Strasberg hide their charms from William Holden and Cliff Robertson , who look equally concerned about their own situation!

I'LL CRY TOMORROW
M-G-M

- **Costume Design (Black-and-white):** Helen Rose

Jo Van Fleet disapproves of Susan Hayward's love for Ray Danton.

Love is a Many Splendored Thing
20th Century-Fox

- **Costume Design (Color):** Charles LeMaire
- **Music (Song):** "Love is a Many Splendored Thing." Music by Sammy Fain. Lyrics by Paul Francis Webster.
- **Music (Scoring of a Dramatic or Comedy Picture):** Alfred Newman

William Holden finds forbidden love in the arms of Jennifer Jones.

Oklahoma
Hornblow, Magna

- **Sound Recording:** Todd-AO Sound Department; Fred Hynes, sound director.
- **Music (Scoring of a Musical Picture):** Robert Russell Bennett, Jay Blackton and Adolph Deutsch

Gene Nelson, Gordon MacRae, Shirley Jones, Charlotte Greenwood, and J.C. Flippen enjoy a beautiful Oklahoma morning.

The Bridges at Toko-Ri
Paramount

- **Special Effects**

The Korean War is the setting for this film, in which William Holden must leave wife Grace Kelly and fly on dangerous missions for his country.

Speedy Gonzales
Warner Brothers

- **Short Subject (Cartoon):** Edward Selzer, producer

Survival City
20th Century-Fox

- **Short Subject (One-reel):** Edmund Reek, producer

The Face of Lincoln
University of Southern California, Cavalcade Pictures

- **Short Subject:** Wilbur T. Blume, producer

Men Against the Arctic
Disney, Buena Vista

- **Documentary (Short Subjects):** Walt Disney, producer

Helen Keller in Her Story
Nancy Hamilton Presentation

- **Documentary (Features):** Nancy Hamilton, producer

Samurai, The Legend of Musashi
Japanese

- **Honorary Award:** Best foreign language film first released in the United States in 1955.

1956

AROUND THE WORLD IN 80 DAYS
Todd, United Artists

- **Best Picture:** Produced by Michael Todd
- **Writing (Best Screenplay – adapted):** James Poe, John Farrow and S.J. Perelman
- **Cinematography (Color):** Lionel Lindon
- **Film Editing:** Gene Ruggiero and Paul Weatherwax
- **Music (Scoring of a Dramatic or Comedy Picture):** Victor Young

THE KING AND I
20th Century-Fox

- **Best Actor:** Yul Brynner
- **Art Direction–Set Decoration (Color):** Lyle R. Wheeler and John DeCuir; Walter M. Scott and Paul S. Fox
- **Costume Design (Color):** Irene Sharaff
- **Sound Recording:** Carl Faulkner, sound director, 20th Century Fox Studio Sound Dept.
- **Music (Scoring of a Musical):** Alfred Newman and Ken Darby

Cantinflas and David Niven meet Marlene Dietrich and Frank Sinatra in a saloon / dance hall near the end of their difficult trip.

Yul Brynner listens to, judges, and initially controls Deborah Kerr before she takes over in this famous musical.

ANASTASIA
20ᵀᴴ CENTURY-FOX

- **Best Actress:** Ingrid Bergman

In this lobby card, Yul Brynner is just not sure whether Ingrid Bergman is an impostor or the real daughter of the former Czar Nicholas II. Note Akim Tamiroff and Felix Aylmer on the left. This was Ingrid Bergman's first American film in six years.

WRITTEN ON THE WIND
Universal - International

- **Best Supporting Actress:** Dorothy Malone

Left to right: Rock Hudson, Lauren Bacall, Robert Stack, and Dorothy Malone star in an unhappy love tale.

LUST FOR LIFE
M-G-M

- **Best Supporting Actor:** Anthony Quinn

Kirk Douglas as Van Gogh and Anthony Quinn as Gauguin .

GIANT
Warner Brothers

- **Direction:** George Stevens

French lobby color still shows the three main stars of this film: Elizabeth Taylor, Rock Hudson, and James Dean.

THE BRAVE ONE
King Brothers, RKO Radio

- **Writing (Motion Picture Story):** Dalton Trumbo (AKA Robert Rich)

Michael Ray wants to save his pet bull from being killed in the bull ring. Frank Silvera looks on approvingly.

THE RED BALLOON
Lopert Films (French)

- **Writing (Best Screenplay-Original):** Albert Lamorisse

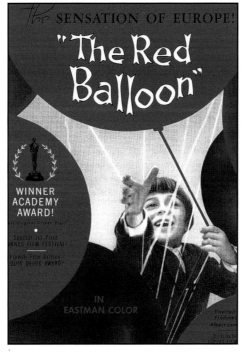

A large red balloon and a little boy in Paris become friends. Based on the book "The Red Balloon," by Albert Lamorisse.

SOMEBODY UP THERE LIKES ME
M-G-M

- **Cinematography (Black-and-white):** Joseph Ruttenberg
- **Art Direction–Set Decoration (Black-and-white):** Cedric Gibbons and Malcolm F. Brown; Edwin B. Willis and F. Keogh Gleason

Paul Newman, as Rocky Graziano, seems more concerned about his boxing than he is about his relationship with Pier Angeli.

THE SOLID GOLD CADILLAC
Columbia

- **Costume Design (Black-and-white):** Jean Louis

Judy Holliday outwits Paul Douglas in this comedy about shenanigans in corporate life.

THE TEN COMMANDMENTS
DeMille, Paramount

- **Special Effects:** John Fulton

Yul Brynner (as Pharaoh) and Anne Baxter are amused by Charlton Heston (as Moses).

THE MAN WHO KNEW TOO MUCH
Hitchcock, Paramount

- **Music:** "Whatever Will Be, Will Be (Que Sera, Sera)." Music and lyrics by Jay Livingston and Ray Evans

Doris Day and James Stewart rescue their son and thwart an assassination in this Alfred Hitchcock thriller.

MISTER MAGOO'S PUDDLE JUMPER
UPA, Columbia

- **Short Subject (Cartoon):** Stephen Bosustow, producer

CRASHING THE WATER BARRIER
Warner Brothers

- **Short Subject (One-reel):** Konstantin Kalser, producer

THE BESPOKE OVERCOAT
George K. Arthur, Go Pictures, Inc.

- **Short Subject:** Romulus Films, Producer

THE TRUE STORY OF THE CIVIL WAR
Camera Eye Pictures

- **Documentary (Short Subject):** Louis Clyde Stoumen, producer

THE SILENT WORLD
Filmad-F.S.J.Y.C., Columbia (French)

- **Documentary (Feature):** Jacques-Yves Cousteau, producer

Jacques-Yves Cousteau explores the world beneath the sea.

LA STRADA
Italy

- **Foreign Language Film:** Dino DeLaurentis and Carlo Ponti, producers

Gulietta Masina and Anthony Quinn, shown both in the photo and in the border art, star in this Federico Fellini film, a bittersweet story about carnival life. (Mexican lobby card)

THE BRIDGE ON THE RIVER KWAI

Horizon, Columbia

- **Best Picture:** Produced by Sam Spiegel
- **Best Actor:** Alec Guinness
- **Direction:** David Lean
- **Writing (Screenplay based on material from another medium):** Pierre Boulle, Carl Foreman, and Michael Wilson
- **Cinematography:** Jack Hildyard
- **Film Editing:** Peter Taylor
- **Music (Music Scoring):** Malcolm Arnold

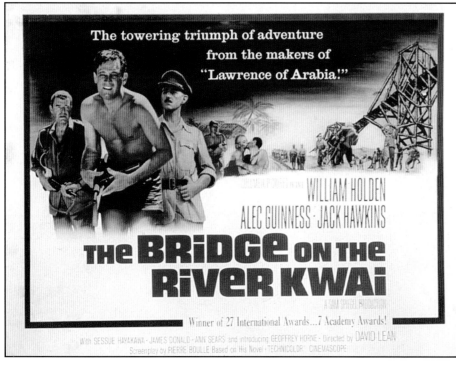

This re-release title lobby card shows all of the stars, as well as the bridge. The original cards did not show the stars together. Left to right: Jack Hawkins, William Holden, Alec Guinness, Ann Sears, and Sessue Hayakawa.

THE THREE FACES OF EVE

20th Century-Fox

- **Best Actress:** Joanne Woodward

Joanne Woodward shows one of her three personalities to David Wayne.

SAYONARA

Goetz, Warner Brothers

- **Best Supporting Actor:** Red Buttons
- **Best Supporting Actress:** Miyoshi Umeki
- **Art Direction-Set Decoration:** Ted Haworth; Robert Priestly
- **Sound Recording:** Warner Brothers Studio Sound Department - George Groves, sound director

Pilot Marlon Brando falls in love with actress Miiko Taka, while award winners Miyoshi Umeki and Red Buttons also fall in love, but with tragic results.

DESIGNING WOMAN
M-G-M

- **Writing (Story and Screenplay written directly for the screen):** George Wells

Stormy marriage between sportswriter Gregory Peck and fashion designer Lauren Bacall.

LES GIRLS
Siegel, M-G-M

- **Costume Design:** Orry-Kelly

Mitzi Gaynor, Kay Kendall, and Taina Elg sing and dance with Gene Kelly.

THE ENEMY BELOW
20th Century-Fox

- **Special Effects:** Walter Rossi

World War II submarine movie pits American commander Robert Mitchum against German commander Curt Jurgens.

THE JOKER IS WILD
Paramount

- **Music (Song):** "All the Way." Music by James Van Heusen. Lyrics by Sammy Cahn.

Jeanne Crain and Frank Sinatra in this musical biography of Joe E. Lewis.

Birds Anonymous
Warner Brothers

- **Short Subject (Cartoon):** Edward Selzer, producer

The Wetback Hound
Disney, Buena Vista

- **Short Subjects (Live Action Subjects):** Larry Lansburgh, producer

Hound and deer are pals facing the elements.

Albert Schweitzer
Hill and Anderson Prod., Louis De Rochemont Associates.

- **Documentary (Feature):** Jerome Hill, producer

This historical feature was narrated by Burgess Meredith and Fredric March.

The Nights of Cabiria
Italy

- **Foreign Language Film**

Gulietta Masina as a Roman prostitute in this Fellini film.

1958

GIGI
M-G-M, Freed

- **Best Picture:** Produced by Arthur Freed
- **Direction:** Vincente Minnelli
- **Writing (Screenplay based on material from another medium):** Alan Jay Lerner
- **Cinematography (Color):** Joseph Ruttenberg
- **Art Direction-Set Decoration (Black-and-white or Color):** William A. Horning and Preston Ames; Henry Grace and Keogh Gleason.
- **Costume Design (Black-and-white or Color):** Cecil Beaton
- **Film Editing:** Adrienne Fazan
- **Music (Song):** "Gigi." Music by Frederick Loewe. Lyrics by Alan Jay Lerner.
- **Music (Scoring of a Musical Picture):** Andre Previn

This re-release lobby card shows Louis Jourdan, Leslie Caron, and Maurice Chevalier in a wonderful musical set in Paris.

SEPARATE TABLES
Hecht-Hill-Lancaster, United Artists

- **Best Actor:** David Niven
- **Best Supporting Actress:** Wendy Hiller

Left to right: David Niven, Gladys Cooper, Deborah Kerr, Rita Hayworth, Cathleen Nesbitt, and Burt Lancaster exchange looks from their separate tables.

Rita Hayworth is provoked by Wendy Hiller.

I Want To Live
Figaro, United Artists

- **Best Actress:** Susan Hayward

Susan Hayward, shown here in a not-so-typical jail uniform.

The Big Country
Anthony-Worldwide, United Artists

- **Best Supporting Actor:** Burl Ives

The Defiant Ones
Kramer, United Artists

- **Writing (Story and Screenplay written directly for the screen):** Nedrick Young and Harold Jacob Smith
- **Cinematography (Black-and-white):** Sam Leavitt

Sidney Poitier and Tony Curtis attempt their prison escape.

What a cast! The musical score by Jerome Moross is unforgettable. Left to right: Charles Bickford, Charlton Heston, Carroll Baker, Gregory Peck, Jean Simmons, Burl Ives, and Chuck Connors.

SOUTH PACIFIC
Magna Corporation, 20th Century-Fox

- **Sound:** Todd-AO Sound Department, Fred Hynes, sound director.

John Kerr stands by, while Mitzi Gaynor and Rossano Brazzi try to work out their love for one another.

TOM THUMB
Pal, M-G-M

- **Special Effects:** Tom Howard

June Thorburn gives advice to Russ Tamblyn (as Tom Thumb) in this amusing children's film.

THE OLD MAN AND THE SEA
Hayward, Warner Brothers

- **Music (Scoring of a Dramatic or Comedy Picture):** Dimitri Tiomkin

Spencer Tracy battles the sea in this Hemingway classic.

KNIGHTY KNIGHT BUGS
Warner Brothers

- **Short Subject (Cartoon):** John W. Burton, producer

GRAND CANYON
Walt Disney Productions, Buena Vista

- **Short Subject (Live Action Subject):** Walt Disney, producer

AMA GIRLS
Disney Productions, Buena Vista

- **Documentary (Short Subject):** Ben Sharpsteen, producer

Japanese pearl divers clean oysters.

WHITE WILDERNESS
Disney Productions, Buena Vista

- **Documentary (Feature):** Ben Sharpsteen, producer

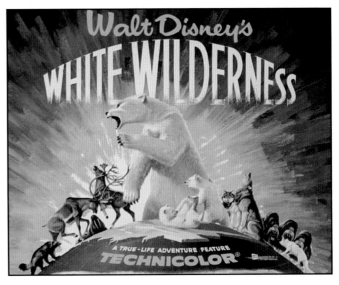

An Arctic adventure film!

MY UNCLE (MON ONCLE)
France

- **Foreign Language Film**

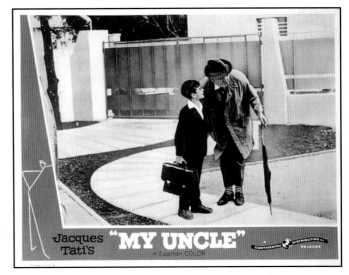

Many silent gags are used in the Jacques Tati French classic. That is Tati at right.

1959

Ben Hur
M-G-M

- **Best Picture:** Produced by Sam Zimbalist
- **Best Actor:** Charlton Heston
- **Best Supporting Actor:** Hugh Griffith
- **Direction:** William Wyler
- **Cinematography (Color):** Robert L. Surtees
- **Art Direction-Set Decoration (Color):** William A. Horning and Edward Carfagno, Hugh Hunt
- **Costume Design (Color):** Elizabeth Haffenden
- **Sound:** Franklin E. Milton
- **Film Editing:** Ralph E. Winters and John D. Dunning
- **Special Effects:** A. Arnold Gillespie, Robert McDonald and Milo Lory
- **Music (Story of a Dramatic or Comedy Picture):** Miklos Rozsa

Best supporting actor Hugh Griffith was not pictured on any first release lobby cards, but when the film was re-released in 1969, Griffith got his due. He is shown here with Best Actor Charlton Heston.

Room at the Top
Romulus, Continental (British)

- **Best Actress:** Simone Signoret
- **Writing (Screenplay based on material from another medium):** Neil Paterson

Simone Signoret suspects Laurence Harvey of infidelity.

The Diary of Anne Frank
20th Century Fox

- **Cinematography (Black-and-white):** William C. Mellor
- **Art Direction-Set Decoration (Black-and-white):** Lyle R. Wheeler and George W. Davis; Walter M. Scott and Stuart A. Reiss

The only lobby card to show the principal cast! Left to right: Ed Wynn, Millie Perkins, Richard Beymer, Lou Jacobi, Diane Baker, and Shelley Winters.

PILLOW TALK
Arwin, Universal - International

- **Writing (Story and screenplay written directly for the screen):** Russell Rouse, Clarence Greene, Stanley Shapiro, and Maurice Richlin.

In this film, Doris Day and Rock Hudson provide the romance, while Tony Randall and Thelma Ritter provide the comedy.

A HOLE IN THE HEAD
Sincap, United Artists

- **Music:** "High Hopes." Music by James Van Heusen. Lyrics by Sammy Cahn.

Frank Sinatra hugs Eddie Hodges, while supporting cast Carolyn Jones, Thelma Ritter, Eleanor Parker, Edward G. Robinson, and Keenan Wynn observe.

SOME LIKE IT HOT
Mirisch-Ashton, United Artists

- **Costume Design (Black-and-white):** Orry-Kelly

This famous and oft used image shows Marilyn Monroe with her two co-stars, Tony Curtis and Jack Lemmon.

PORGY AND BESS
Goldwyn, Columbia

- **Music (Scoring of a Musical Picture):** Andre Previn and Ken Darby

Dorothy Dandridge, Sammy Davis Jr., and Sidney Poitier as Porgy star in this famous "Catfish Row" musical. (Mini-window Card)

Moonbird
Storyboard – Harrison

- **Short Subject (Cartoon):** John Hubley, producer

The Golden Fish
Les Requins Associes, Columbia (French)

- **Short Subject (Live Action Subject):** Jacques-Yves Cousteau

The cat definitely wants the fish!

Glass
Netherlands Government, George K. Arthur, Go Pictures (The Netherlands)

- **Documentary (Short Subject):** Bert Haanstra, producer

Serengeti Shall Not Die
Okapia-Film Productions, Transocean Film (German)

- **Documentary (Feature):** Bernhard Grzimek, producer

That fascinating zebra plane fits right in with its surroundings both in the film and on this lively lobby card.

Black Orpheus
France

- **Foreign Language Film**

Marpessa Dawn gazes lovingly at Bruno Mello before the carnival in Rio de Janeiro.

1960

THE APARTMENT
Mirisch, United Artists

- **Best Picture:** Produced by Billy Wilder
- **Direction:** Billy Wilder
- **Writing (Story and screenplay written directly for the screen):** Billy Wilder and I.A.L. Diamond
- **Art Direction–Set Decoration (Black-and-white):** Alexander Trauner and Edward G. Boyle
- **Film Editing:** Daniel Mandell

Wonderful comedy/love story that solidified the careers of Jack Lemmon and Shirley MacLaine.

ELMER GANTRY
Lancaster-Brooks, United Artists

- **Best Actor:** Burt Lancaster
- **Best Supporting Actress:** Shirley Jones
- **Writing:** Richard Brooks

Jean Simmons prays for the soul of Burt Lancaster (as Gantry), while prostitute Shirley Jones tempts him.

BUTTERFIELD 8
Afton-Linebrook, M-G-M

- **Best Actress:** Elizabeth Taylor

Left to right: Eddie Fisher, Susan Oliver, and Elizabeth Taylor in this story of a wayward girl who wishes to turn her life around.

SONS AND LOVERS

Wald, 20ᵗʰ Century-Fox

- **Cinematography (Black-and-white):** Freddie Francis

SPARTACUS

Byrna, Universal – International

- **Best Supporting Actor:** Peter Ustinov
- **Cinematography (Color):** Russell Metty
- **Art Direction–Set Decoration (Color):** Alexander Golitzen and Eric Orbom; Russell A. Gausman and Julia Heron
- **Costume Design (Color):** Valles and Bill Thomas

Wendy Hiller intervenes and attempts to restrain her son, Dean Stockwell, from fighting his father, Trevor Howard.

Serving wenches please Peter Ustinov and Charles Laughton in this historical epic of the gladiator rebellion against Rome.

THE FACTS OF LIFE
Panama and Frank Productions, United Artists

• **Costume Design (Black-and-white):** Edith Head and Edward Stevenson

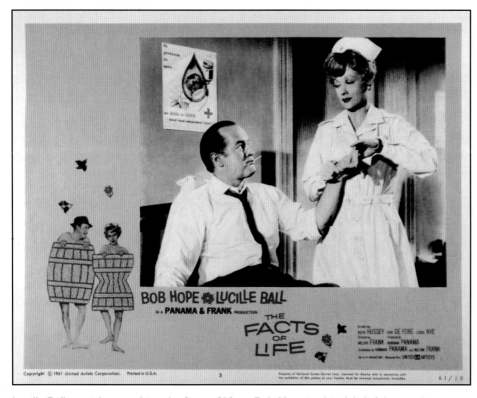

Lucille Ball considers teaching the facts of life to Bob Hope in this delightful comedy.

THE ALAMO
Batjac, United Artists

• **Sound:** Gordon E. Sawyer (Goldwyn), and Fred Hynes (Todd-AO)

This is the only lobby card in the eight card set which shows all three principals: Richard Widmark, John Wayne, and Laurence Harvey. In this scene, the decision of whether or not to take on Santa Anna and three thousand men is being made.

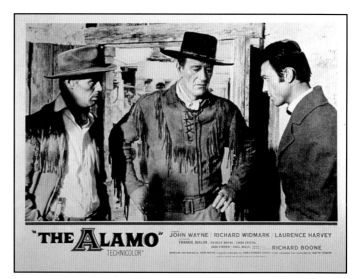

THE TIME MACHINE
Pal, M-G-M

• **Special Effects:** Gene Warren and Tim Baar

Rod Taylor and Yvette Mimieux battle the Morlocks underground as he seeks to return to the time machine.

Never on Sunday
Melinafilm, Lopert Pictures (Greek)

- **Music (Song):** "Never on Sunday." Music and lyrics by Manos Hadjidakis.

A Greek prostitute, as portrayed by Melina Mercouri.

Exodus
Preminger, United Artists

- **Music (Scoring of a Dramatic or Comedy Picture):** Ernest Gold

Ill-fated young lovers Sal Mineo and Jill Haworth take a break from fighting Palestinians.

Song Without End
Goetz, Columbia

- **Music (Scoring of a Musical Picture):** Morris Stoloff and Harry Sukman

Dirk Bogarde, Genevieve Page, Martita Hunt, and Capucine star in this biography of Franz Liszt.

MUNRO
Rembrandt Films, Film Representations

- **Short Subject (Cartoon):** William L. Snyder, producer

DAY OF THE PAINTER
Little Movies, Kingsley-Union Films

- **Short Subject (Live Action Subject):** Ezra R. Baker, producer

GIUSEPPINA
Schoenfeld Films (British)

- **Documentary (Short Subject):** James Hill, Producer

THE HORSE WITH THE FLYING TAIL
Disney, Buena Vista

- **Documentary (Feature):** Larry Lansburgh, producer

THE VIRGIN SPRING
Sweden

- **Foreign Language Film**

POLLYANNA
Disney, Buena Vista

- **Honorary Award:** Hayley Mills for the outstanding juvenile performance of 1960

Happy film starring Richard Egan and Hayley Mills. If you search you will also find Agnes Moorehead, Adolphe Menjou, Karl Malden, Jane Wyman, and Nancy Olson.

In this Ingmar Bergman film, Max Von Sydow comforts his daughter, who has been raped.

1961

WEST SIDE STORY

United Artists, Mirisch Pictures – Seven Arts Productions

- **Best Picture:** Produced by Robert Wise
- **Best Supporting Actor:** George Chakiris
- **Best Supporting Actress:** Rita Moreno
- **Direction:** Robert Wise and Jerome Robbins
- **Cinematography (Color):** Daniel L. Fapp
- **Art Direction–Set Decoration (Color):** Boris Leven; Victor A. Gangelin
- **Costume Design (Color):** Irene Sharaff
- **Sound:** Todd-AO Sound Dept., Fred Hynes, sound director; and Samuel Goldwyn Studio Sound Dept., Gordon E. Sawyer, sound director.
- **Film Editing:** Thomas Stanford
- **Music (Scoring of a Musical Picture):** Saul Chaplin, Johnny Green, Sid Ramin, and Irwin Kostal

Rita Moreno and the Shark ladies show off their dance moves. (Re-release lobby card)

George Chakiris and the Sharks get ready to rumble. (Re-release lobby card)

JUDGEMENT AT NUREMBURG
Kramer, United Artists

- **Best Actor:** Maximillian Schell
- **Writing (Screenplay based on material from another medium):** Abby Mann

Defense attorney Maximilian Schell (left) defends German war criminals while U.S. Prosecutor Richard Widmark looks for an advantage.

SPLENDOR IN THE GRASS
Kazan, Warner Brothers

- **Writing (Story and Screenplay written directly for the screen):** William Inge

In real life, Warren Beatty and Natalie Wood fell in love while making this wonderful film.

TWO WOMEN
Ponti, Embassy (Italian)

- **Best Actress:** Sophia Loren

Jean Paul Belmondo wants to help Sophia Loren and her daughter.

THE HUSTLER
Rossen, 20th Century-Fox

- **Cinematography (Black-and-white):** Eugen Shuftan
- **Art Direction–Set Decoration (Black-and-white):** Harry Horner; Gene Callahan

This cult classic features Paul Newman (as hustler Fast Eddie Felson), who is out-hustled by Jackie Gleason (as Minnesota Fats).

La Dolce Vita
Astor Pictures (Italian)

- **Costume Design (Black-and-white):** Piero Gherardi

In this Federico Fellini classic, Reporter Marcello Mastroianni observes the good life.

The Guns of Navarone
Foreman, Columbia

- **Special Effects:** Bill Warrington and Vivien C. Greenham

Left to right: Soldiers Anthony Quinn, Stanley Baker, Gregory Peck, David Niven, and James Darren consider executing Gia Scala, who might stop their mission.

Breakfast at Tiffany's
Jurow-Shepherd, Paramount

- **Music (Song):** "Moon River." Music by Henry Mancini. Lyrics by Johnny Mercer.
- **Music (Scoring of a Dramatic or Comedy Picture):** Henry Mancini

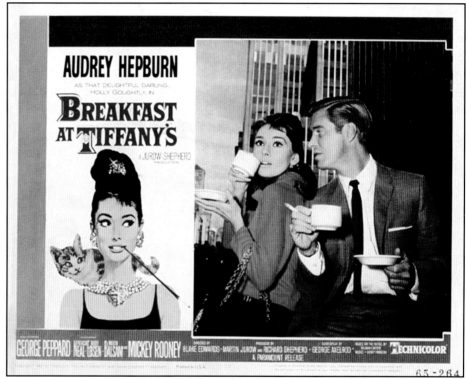

A romantic comedy in New York City with Audrey Hepburn (as Holly GoLightly) and George Peppard, who wishes to reform her from her "escort service" ways. Great drawing of Audrey and her feline friend. Note the original lobby card dated 1961, which was reused in 1965. This was quite common, as National Screen Service and the Independent Poster Exchanges would lease posters. They would be returned by the theatres and then leased again.

ERSATZ (THE SUBSTITUTE)
Zagreb Film, Herts-Lion International Corporation

- **Short Subject (Cartoon)**

SEAWARDS THE GREAT SHIPS
Templar Film Studios, Schoenfeld Films

- **Short Subject (Live Action Subject)**

PROJECT HOPE
Klaeger Films

- **Documentary (Short Subject):** Frank P. Bibas, producer

THE SKY ABOVE, THE MUD BELOW (LE CIEL ET LA BOUE)
Rank Films (French)

- **Documentary (Feature):** Arthur Cohn and Rene Lafuite, producers

Life in Dutch New Guinea is the subject of this documentary film.

THROUGH A GLASS DARKLY
Sweden

- **Foreign Language Film**

Harriet Andersson, just released from a mental institution, has trouble with husband Max Von Sydow.

A FORCE IN READINESS
U.S. Marine Corps

- **Honorary Award:** William L. Hendricks for his patriotic service in bringing this Marine Corps film to the screen, and for bringing honor to the Academy and the motion picture industry as a result.

1962

LAWRENCE OF ARABIA
Horizon-Spiegel-Lean, Columbia

- **Best Picture:** Produced by Sam Spiegel
- **Direction:** David Lean
- **Cinematography (Color):** Fred A. Young
- **Music (Music Score-substantially original):** Maurice Jarre
- **Art Direction–Set Decoration (Color):** John Box and John Stoll; Dario Simoni
- **Sound:** Shepperton Studio; John Cox, sound director
- **Film Editing:** Ann Coates

British soldier Peter O'Toole (as T.E. Lawrence) lobbies for support, as a skeptical Arab Bedouin Chief, played by Anthony Quinn, looks on.

TO KILL A MOCKINGBIRD
Pakula-Mulligan-Brentwood, Universal - International

- **Best Actor:** Gregory Peck
- **Writing (Screenplay based on material from another medium):** Horton Foote
- **Art Direction–Set Decoration (Black-and-white):** Alexander Golitzen and Henry Bumstead; Oliver Emert

Public Defender Gregory Peck defends a man accused of rape, while Peck's children (John Magna, Phillip Alford, and Mary Badham) lend support outside the jail.

THE MIRACLE WORKER
Playfilms, United Artists

- **Best Actress:** Anne Bancroft
- **Best Supporting Actress:** Patty Duke

Anne Bancroft, left, frantically does sign language with Patty Duke (as deaf-mute Helen Keller) in an attempt to communicate.

SWEET BIRD OF YOUTH
Roxbury, M-G-M

- **Best Supporting Actor:** Ed Begley

Ed Begley and Shirley Knight in this Tennessee Williams classic.

DIVORCE – ITALIAN STYLE
Embassy Pictures (Italian)

- **Writing (Story and Screenplay written directly for the screen):** Ennio de Concini, Alfredo Giannetti, and Pierto Germi

Marcello Mastroianni juggles several women in this delightful comedy.

THE LONGEST DAY
Zanuck, 20th Century-Fox

- **Cinematography (Black-and-White):** Jean Bourgoin and Walter Wottitz
- **Special Effects:** Robert MacDonald and Jacques Maumont

Soldiers Robert Wagner, Tommy Sands, and Fabian get ready to land on the beaches of Normandy on what was certainly a long day.

THE DAYS OF WINE AND ROSES
Manulis-Jalem, Warner Brothers

- **Music (Song):** "Days of Wine and Roses." Music by Henry Mancini. Lyrics by Johnny Mercer.

Jack Lemmon tries to kick the drinking habit while his modestly sympathetic wife Lee Remick looks on. Later on, their roles are reversed.

THE MUSIC MAN
Warner Brothers

- **Music (Scoring of Music–adaptation or treatment):** Ray Heindorf

Shirley Jones, Robert Preston, and Buddy Hackett sing and dance in this famous musical.

WHATEVER HAPPENED TO BABY JANE?
Seven Arts-Aldrich, Warner Brothers

- **Costume Design (Black-and-white):** Norma Koch

Betty Davis (as Baby Jane) torments her sister, Joan Crawford.

THE WONDERFUL WORLD OF THE BROTHERS GRIMM
M-G-M and Cinerama

- **Costume Design (Color):** Mary Wills

Claire Bloom and Laurence Harvey watch the puppets perform in the toy shop.

THE HOLE
Storyboard, Inc., Brandon Films

- **Short Subject (Cartoon):** John and Faith Hubley, producers

HEUREUX ANNIVERSAIRE (HAPPY ANNIVERSARY)
Atlantic Pictures (French)

- **Short Subject (Live Action Subject):** Pierre Etaix and J.C. Carriere, producers

DYLAN THOMAS
TWW Ltd., Janus Films (Welsh)

- **Documentary (Short Subject):** Jack Howells, producer

BLACK FOX
Image Productions, Heritage Films

- **Documentary:** Louis Clyde Stoumen, producer

SUNDAYS AND CYBELE
France

- **Foreign Language Film**

Lonely Hardy Kruger finds love and friendship with little girl Patricia Gozzi.

Tough documentary film about the life of Adolph Hitler.

1963

TOM JONES
Woodfall, United Artists-Lopert (British)

- **Best Picture:** Produced by Tony Richardson
- **Direction:** Tony Richardson
- **Writing (Screenplay based on material from another medium):** John Osborne
- **Music (Music Score–Substantially Original):** John Addison

LILIES OF THE FIELD
Rainbow, United Artists

- **Best Actor:** Sidney Poitier

An exuberant Sidney Poitier in the role of a handyman for a group of nuns in Arizona.

Albert Finney conquers yet another amour, Joan Greenwood.

163

HUD
Salem-Dover, Paramount

- **Best Actress:** Patricia Neal
- **Best Supporting Actor:** Melvyn Douglas
- **Cinematography (Black-and-white):** James Wong Howe

Paul Newman pursues the family housekeeper, Patricia Neal.

Paul Newman (left) , Melvyn Douglas, Yvette Vickers, and Brandon deWilde interact in the café.

THE V.I.P.s
M-G-M

- **Best Supporting Actress:** Margaret Rutherford

Two V.I.P.'s, Orson Welles and Margaret Rutherford, meet in this film.

How the West Was Won

M-G-M and Cinerama

- **Writing (Story and Screenplay written directly for the screen):** James R. Webb
- **Sound:** Franklin E. Milton, sound director, M-G-M Studio Sound Dept.
- **Film Editing:** Harold F. Kress

Cleopatra

Wanger, 20th Century-Fox

- **Cinematography (Color):** Leon Shamroy
- **Art Direction-Set Decoration (Color):** John DeCuir, Jack Martin Smith, Hilyard Brown, Herman Blumenthal, Elven Webb, Maurice Pelling and Boris Juraga; Walter M. Scott, Paul S. Fox, and Ray Moyer
- **Costume Design (Color):** Irene Sharaff, Vittorio Nino Novarese and Renie
- **Special Visual Effects:** Emil Kosa Jr.

What a cast!

Elizabeth Taylor, as Cleopatra, seduces in turn both Rex Harrison (as Caesar) and Richard Burton (as Marc Antony) in this four-hour epic which includes the joining of Rome and Egypt.

America, America
Kazan, Warner Brothers

- **Art Direction–Set Decoration (Black-and-white):** Gene Callahan

A cast unknown to American audiences is ably directed by Elia Kazan in this story about immigration to the United States.

Federico Fellini's 8 1/2
Embassy Pictures (Italian)

- **Costume Design (Black-and-white):** Piero Gherardi
- **Foreign Language Film**

Movie director Marcello Mastroianni romances Sandra Milo.

It's a Mad, Mad, Mad, Mad World
Kramer, United Artists

- **Sound Effects:** Walter G. Elliott

A madcap comedy starring, left to right, Edie Adams, Sid Caesar, Jonathan Winters, Dorothy Provine, Ethel Merman, Milton Berle, Mickey Rooney, and Buddy Hackett.

PAPA'S DELICATE CONDITION
Amro, Paramount

- **Music (Song):** "Call Me Irresponsible." Music by James Van Heusen. Lyrics by Sammy Cahn.

Glynis Johns puts up with papa Jackie Gleason's antics. He is shown with screen daughter Linda Bruhl in his arms.

IRMA LA DOUCE
Mirisch-Alperson, United Artists

- **Music (Scoring of Music–adaptation or treatment):** Andre Previn

Jack Lemmon falls in love with French prostitute Shirley MacLaine in this film, one of their best together.

THE CRITIC
Pintoff -Crossbow Productions, Columbia

- **Short Subject (Cartoon):** Ernest Pintoff, producer

One of Mel Brooks's earliest successes.

AN OCCURRENCE AT OWL CREEK BRIDGE
Janus Films

- **Short Subject (Live Action Subject):** Paul de Roubaix and Marcel Ichac, producers

CHAGALL
Auerbach – Flag Films

- **Documentary (Short Subject):** Simon Schiffrin, producer

ROBERT FROST: A LOVER'S QUARREL WITH THE WORLD
WGBH Educational Foundation

- **Documentary (Feature):** Robert Hughes, producer

MY FAIR LADY
Warner Brothers

- **Best Picture:** Produced by Jack L. Warner
- **Best Actor:** Rex Harrison
- **Direction:** George Cukor
- **Cinematography (Color):** Harry Stradling
- **Art Direction–Set Decoration (Color):** Gene Allen and Cecil Beaton; George James Hopkins
- **Costume Design (Color):** Cecil Beaton
- **Sound:** George R. Groves, sound director, Warner Bros. Studio Sound Dept.
- **Music (Scoring of Music–adaptation or treatment):** Andre Previn

MARY POPPINS
Disney, Buena Vista

- **Best Actress:** Julie Andrews
- **Film Editing:** Cotton Warburton
- **Special Visual Effects:** Peter Ellenshaw, Hamilton Luske and Eustace Lycett
- **Music (Song):** "Chim Chim Cher-ee." Music and lyrics by Richard M. Sherman and Robert B. Sherman
- **Music (Music Score–Substantially Original):** Richard M. Sherman and Robert B. Sherman

This re-release lobby card shows the two principals in a musical version of "Pygmalion." Rex Harrison plays Professor Henry Higgins, who takes the impoverished Liza Doolittle, played by Audrey Hepburn, and makes her into a lady.

Dick Van Dyke (as Bert, the chimney sweep), Karen Dotrice, Matthew Garber, and Julie Andrews (as Mary Poppins) dance and sing on the roofs of London.

TOPKAPI
Filmways, United Artists

- **Best Supporting Actor:** Peter Ustinov

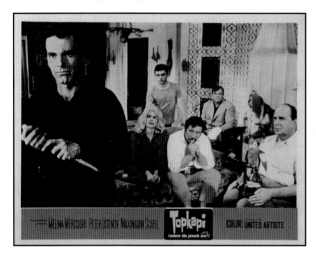

Left to right: Maximilian Schell, Melina Mercouri, Despo Diamantidou, Peter Ustinov, and Robert Morley plan a robbery in Istanbul.

ZORBA, THE GREEK
Rochley, International Classics/20th Century-Fox

- **Best Supporting Actress:** Lila Kedrova
- **Cinematography (Black-and-white):** Walter Lassally
- **Art Direction–Set Decoration (Black-and-white):** Vassilis Fotopoulos

Alan Bates (left) and Anthony (Zorba) Quinn share an odd-couple relationship.

BECKET
Wallis, Paramount

- **Writing (Screenplay based on material from another medium):** Edward Anhalt

Peter O'Toole as King Henry II, and Richard Burton as Beckett, Archbishop of Canterbury, talk about sharing various duties and pleasures.

FATHER GOOSE
Granox, Universal

- **Writing (Story and Screenplay written directly for the screen):** S.H. Barnett, Peter Stone, and Frank Tarloff

Cary Grant shares his scotch with Leslie Caron.

THE NIGHT OF THE IGUANA
Seven Arts, M-G-M

- **Costume Design (Black-and-white):** Dorothy Jeakins

Top to bottom: Ava Gardner, Deborah Kerr, Richard Burton, and Sue Lyon in a film touching on the ups and downs of life.

GOLDFINGER
Broccoli-Saltzman-Eon, United Artists (British)

- **Sound Effects:** Norman Wanstall

Sean Connery (as James Bond) decides whether to escape from or fall into the clutches of Honor Blackman (as Pussy Galore).

THE PINK PHINK
Mirisch–Geoffrey, United Artists

- **Short Subject (Cartoon):** David H. Depatie and Friz Freleng, producers

CASALS CONDUCTS: 1964
Thalia Films, Beckman Film Corporation

- **Short Subject (Live Action Subject):** Edward Schreiber, producer

NINE FROM LITTLE ROCK
U.S. Information Agency, Guggenheim Productions

- **Documentary:** Short Subject

JACQUES-YVES COUSTEAU'S WORLD WITHOUT SUN
Columbia

- **Documentary (Feature):** Jacques-Yves Cousteau, producer

"Oceanauts" live for one month in an undersea "city" in this Jacques Yves Costeau documentary.

YESTERDAY, TODAY, AND TOMORROW
Italy

- **Foreign Language Film**

Sophia Loren performs a famous striptease in this three-part movie with Marcello Mastroianni.

7 FACES OF DR. LAO
Pal, M-G-M

- **Honorary Award:** William Tuttle, Make-up achievement

Tony Randall (as Dr. Lao), in one of his famous disguises, entertains Barbara Eden and John Ericson.

1965

THE SOUND OF MUSIC
Argyle, 20th CenturyFox

- **Best Picture:** Produced by Robert Wise
- **Direction:** Robert Wise
- **Sound:** 20th Century-Fox Studio Sound Dept., James P. Corcoran, sound director; and Todd A-O Sound Dept., Fred Hynes
- **Film Editing:** William Reynolds
- **Music (Scoring of Music–adaptation or treatment):** Irwin Kostal

Eleanor Parker shocks Julie Andrews with news of her engagement to Christopher Plummer (Baron Von Trapp).

CAT BALLOU
Hecht, Columbia

- **Best Actor:** Lee Marvin

Left to right: Dwayne Hickman. Michael Callan, Lee Marvin, and Tom Nardini support Jane Fonda (Cat Ballou) against the bad guys. Not exactly a tough looking group!

DARLING
Anglo-Amalgamated, Embassy (British)

- **Best Actress:** Julie Christie
- **Writing (Story and Screenplay written directly for the screen):** Frederic Raphael
- **Costume Design (Black-and-white):** Julie Harris

Julie Christie fights her way up the social ladder with Laurence Harvey and Dirk Bogarde, only to find unhappiness.

A Thousand Clowns
Harrell, United Artists

- **Best Supporting Actor:** Martin Balsam

Brothers Jason Robards and Martin Balsam discuss life as only brothers can.

A Patch of Blue
Berman-Green, M-G-M

- **Best Supporting Actress:** Shelley Winters

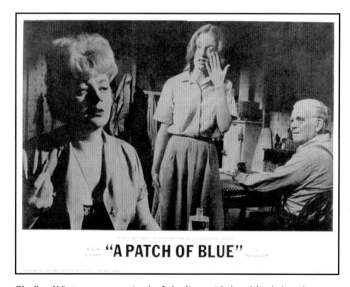

Shelley Winters seems tired of dealing with her blind daughter, Elizabeth Hartman. The dominated husband, Wallace Ford , is appalled.

Doctor Zhivago
Ponti, M-G-M

- **Writing (Screenplay based on material from another medium):** Robert Bolt
- **Cinematography (Color):** Freddie Young
- **Art Direction–Set Decoration (Color):** John Box and Terry Marsh; Dario Simoni
- **Costume Design (Color):** Phyllis Dalton
- **Music (Music Score–Substantially Original):** Maurice Jarre

Julie Christie jealously watches Geraldine Chaplin, who is set to marry Omar Sharif.

SHIP OF FOOLS
Kramer, Columbia

- **Cinematography (Black-and-white):** Ernest Laszlo
- **Art Direction–Set Decoration (Black and White):** Robert Clatworthy; Joseph Kish

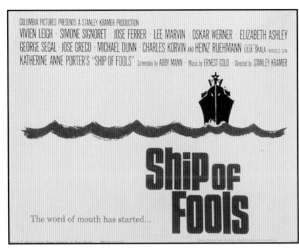

A major cast portraying characters who were indeed foolish in their sad relationships.

THUNDERBALL
Broccoli-Saltzman-McClory, United Artists (British)

- **Special Visual Effects:** John Sears

Sean Connery as James Bond gets a back rub, before reciprocating with interest!

THE GREAT RACE
Patricia-Jalem-Reynard, Warner Brothers

- **Sound Effects:** Tregoweth Brown

Peter Falk, Jack Lemmon, Tony Curtis, Natalie Wood, and Keenan Wynn share the glory of victory in this slapstick classic.

THE SANDPIPER
Filmways-Venice, M-G-M

- **Music (Song):** "The Shadow of Your Smile." Music by Johnny Mandel. Lyrics by Paul Francis Webster.

Richard Burton eyes Elizabeth Taylor with obvious interest.

THE DOT AND THE LINE
M-G-M

- **Short Subject (Cartoon):** Chuck Jones and Les Goldman, producers

THE CHICKEN (LE POULET)
Pathe Contempory Film (French)

- **Short Subject (Live Action Subject):** Claude Berri, producer

TO BE ALIVE
Johnson Wax

- **Documentary (Short Subject):** Francis Thompson, Inc., producer

THE ELEANOR ROOSEVELT STORY
American International

- **Documentary:** Sidney Glazier, producer

An accurate autobiography of the former First Lady.

THE SHOP ON MAIN STREET
Czechoslovakia

- **Foreign Language Film**

Ida Kaminska and Josef Kroner star in this World War II story of persecution and hope.

1966

A Man for all Seasons
Highland Films, Columbia

- **Best Picture:** Produced by Fred Zinnemann
- **Best Actor:** Paul Scofield
- **Direction:** Fred Zinnemann
- **Writing (Screenplay based on material from another medium):** Robert Bolt
- **Cinematography (Color):** Ted Moore
- **Costume Design (Color):** Elizabeth Haffenden and Joan Bridge

Who's Afraid of Virginia Woolf?
Chenault , Warner Brothers

- **Best Actress:** Elizabeth Taylor
- **Best Supporting Actress:** Sandy Dennis
- **Cinematography (Black-and-white):** Haskell Wexler
- **Art Direction–Set Decoration (Black-and-white):** Richard Sylbert; George James Hopkins
- **Costume Design:** Irene Sharaff

Paul Scofield (as Sir Thomas More) visits Orson Welles for religious support against Henry VIII and the newly formed Church of England.

Destructive couple Richard Burton and Elizabeth Taylor entertain naïve newlyweds George Segal and Sandy Dennis.

THE FORTUNE COOKIE
Phalanx-Jalem-Mirsch, United Artists

- **Best Supporting Actor:** Walter Matthau

Shyster Walter Matthau helps brother-in-law Jack Lemmon in an insurance fraud case.

A MAN AND A WOMAN
Les Films 13, Allied Artists (French)

- **Writing (Story and Screenplay written directly for the screen):** Claude Lelouch and Pierre Uytterhoeven
- **Foreign Language Film** (France)

Anouk Aimee and Jean-Louis Trintignant fall in love after losing both of their spouses....but the memories of them still linger.

FANTASTIC VOYAGE
20ᵗʰ Century-Fox

- **Art Direction–Set Decoration (Color):** Jack Martin Smith and Dale Hennessy; Walter M. Scott and Stuart A. Reiss
- **Special Visual Effects:** Art Cruickshank

Reduced to tiny proportions, scientists Racquel Welch, Arthur Kennedy, William Redfield, Donald Pleasence, and Stephen Boyd travel through the bloodstream of an injured man.

GRAND PRIX
Lewis-Frankenheimer-Cherokee, M-G-M

- **Sound:** M-G-M Studio sound department, Franklin E. Milton, sound director
- **Film Editing:** Fredric Steinkamp, Henry Berman, Stewart Linder, and Frank Santillo
- **Sound Effects:** Gordon Daniel

This lobby card says it all. You can almost hear those engines.

BORN FREE
Open Road-Atlas Films, Columbia (British)

- **Music (Song):** " Born Free." Music by John Barry. Lyrics by Don Black.
- **Music (Original Music Score):** John Barry

In this family film, Virginia McKenna and Bill Travers portray two game wardens, who raise and protect lions, befriending a special one named Elsa in the process.

A FUNNY THING HAPPENED ON THE WAY TO THE FORUM
Frank, United Artists

- **Music (Scoring of Music–adaptation or treatment):** Ken Thorne

Zero Mostel woos the fair Jack Gilford in this amusing musical comedy!

HERB ALPERT AND THE TIJUANA BRASS DOUBLE FEATURE
Paramount

- **Short Subject (Cartoon):** John and Faith Hubley, producers

A cartoon featuring the music of Herb Alpert.

WILD WINGS
British Transport Films, Manson Distributing

- **Short Subject (Live Action Subject):** Edgar Anstey, producer

A YEAR TOWARD TOMORROW
Sun Dial Films for the Office of Economic Opportunity

- **Documentary (Short Subject):** Edmond A. Levy, producer

THE WAR GAME
BBC Productions for the British Film Institute, Pathe Contemporary Films

- **Documentary (Feature):** Peter Watkins, Producer

A look at the aftermath of nuclear war.

IN THE HEAT OF THE NIGHT

Mirisch, United Artists

- **Best Picture:** Produced by Walter Mirisch
- **Best Actor:** Rod Steiger
- **Writing (Screenplay based on material from another medium):** Stirling Silliphant
- **Sound:** Samuel Goldwyn Studio Sound Department
- **Film Editing:** Hal Ashby

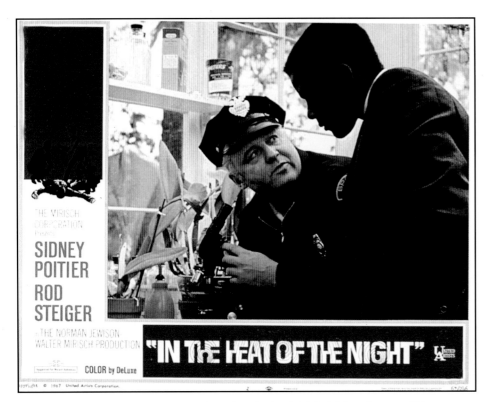

Mississippi police chief Rod Steiger is forced to deal with Philadelphia detective Sidney Poitier.

GUESS WHO'S COMING TO DINNER?

Kramer, Columbia

- **Best Actress:** Katharine Hepburn
- **Writing (Story and Screenplay written directly for the screen):** William Rose

Sidney Poitier and fiancée Katharine Houghton hope for acceptance from parents Katharine Hepburn and Spencer Tracy.

COOL HAND LUKE

Jalem, Warner Brothers – Seven Arts

- **Best Supporting Actor:** George Kennedy

Paul Newman (Luke, with cane) and George Kennedy (far right) contemplate their own plans for escape from a chain gang.

BONNIE AND CLYDE
Tatira-Hiller; Warner Brothers – Seven Arts

- **Best Supporting Actress:** Estelle Parsons
- **Cinematography:** Burnett Guffey

THE GRADUATE
Nichols-Turman, Embassy

- **Direction:** Mike Nichols

This is the only lobby card in the original set that shows Estelle Parsons (as Blanche Barrow). Here she watches her husband, Gene Hackman (as Buck Barrow) die.

In this film, a mother becomes involved with a young neighbor, who then falls in love with her daughter instead. Anne Bancroft (as Mrs. Robinson) finds her lover (Dustin Hoffman) and her daughter (Katharine Ross) together, as shown in this re-release lobby card.

CAMELOT
Warner Brothers – Seven Arts

- **Art Direction–Set Decoration:** John Truscott and Edward Carrere; John W. Brown
- **Costume Design:** John Truscott
- **Music (Scoring of Music–adaptation or treatment):** Alfred Newman and Ken Darby

Unlikely singer Richard Harris (as King Arthur) serenades Vanessa Redgrave (as Guinevere).

DOCTOR DOOLITTLE
Apjac, 20th Century-Fox

- **Special Effects:** L.B. Abbott
- **Music (Song):** "Talk to the Animals." Music and lyrics by Leslie Bricusse.

Rex Harrison, as Dr. Doolittle, doffs his hat while riding through his private zoo.

THE DIRTY DOZEN
Aldrich, M-G-M

- **Sound Effects:** John Poyner

The "Dirty Dozen," U.S. Army prisoners, are all pictured here on this re-release lobby card. Some of them, left to right, include: Clint Walker, Telly Savalas, Jim Brown, Trini Lopez, Donald Sutherland, Charles Bronson, and John Cassavetes. Our apologies to all those not named!

THOROUGHLY MODERN MILLIE
Hunter, Universal

- **Music (Original Music Score):** Elmer Bernstein

James Fox and Julie Andrews watch Carol Channing sing to a confused Jack Soo.

THE BOX
Brandon Films

- **Short Subject (Cartoon):** Fred Wolf, producer

A PLACE TO STAND
T.D.F. Productions for Ontario Department of Economics and Development, Columbia

- **Short Subject (Live Action Subject):** Christopher Chapman, producer

THE REDWOODS
King Screen Productions

- **Documentary (Short Subject):** Mark Harris and Trevor Greenwood, producers

THE ANDERSON PLATOON
French Broadcasting System

- **Documentary (Feature):** Pierre Schoendoerffer, producer

CLOSELY WATCHED TRAINS
Czechoslovakia

- **Foreign Language Film**

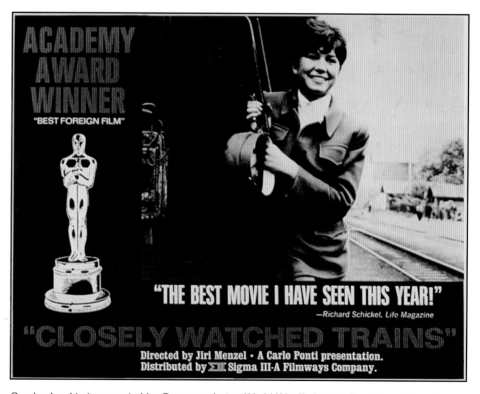

Czechoslovakia is occupied by Germany during World War II. A train dispatcher helps the underground movement.

1968

OLIVER!
Romulus, Columbia

- **Best Picture:** Produced by John Woolf
- **Direction:** Carol Reed
- **Art Direction–Set Decoration:** John Box and Terence Marsh; Vernon Dixon and Ken Muggleston
- **Sound:** Shepperton Studio Sound Department
- **Music (Score of a Musical Picture–original or adaptation):** John Green
- **Honorary Award:** Onna White, for achievement in choreography

Ron Moody (Fagin) compliments Mark Lester (Oliver) on his first theft, which was coached by Jack Wild (The Artful Dodger).

CHARLY
ABC – Selmur, Cinerama

- **Best Actor:** Cliff Robertson

Mentally challenged patient Cliff Robertson, assisted by caseworker Claire Bloom, becomes a brilliant man.

FUNNY GIRL
Rastar, Columbia

- **Best Actress:** Barbra Streisand

Musical biography of Fanny Brice as portrayed by Barbra Streisand, shown here with Omar Sharif.

THE SUBJECT WAS ROSES
M-G-M

• **Best Supporting Actor:** Jack Albertson

Returning soldier Martin Sheen with his parents, Patricia Neal and Jack Albertson.

ROSEMARY'S BABY
Castle, Paramount

• **Best Supporting Actress:** Ruth Gordon

THE LION IN WINTER
Haworth, Avco Embassy

• **Best Actress:** Katharine Hepburn
• **Writing (Screenplay based on material from another medium):** James Goldman
• **Music (Original Score for a motion picture [not a musical]):** John Barry

A spirited exchange between Katharine Hepburn (Eleanor of Aquitaine) and Peter O'Toole (King Henry II).

Unfortunately, the Academy Award® winner, Ruth Gordon, was not shown on a lobby card made for this film. Here is Mia Farrow (as Rosemary) and her on-screen husband, John Cassavetes, who portrays a new member of the film's witch coven.

The Producers
Glazier, Avco Embassy

- **Writing (Story and Screenplay written directly for the screen):** Mel Brooks

Hard-luck Broadway producer Zero Mostel, right, persuades Gene Wilder , left, to invest in his play, while Kenneth Mars listens in.

Romeo and Juliet
B.H.E. Verona-DeLaurentis, Paramount

- **Cinematography:** Pasqualino De Santis
- **Costume Design:** Danilo Donati

Olivia Hussey (Juliet) and Leonard Whiting (Romeo) express love in the famous balcony scene.

Bullitt
Solar, Warner Brothers-Seven Arts

- **Film Editing:** Frank P. Keller

Steve McQueen (Bullitt) is a detective who suspects something is wrong with inspector Robert Vaughn's murder investigation.

2001: A SPACE ODYSSEY
Polaris, M-G-M

- **Special Effects:** Stanley Kubrick

Gary Lockwood and Keir Dullea star in this sci-fi classic, along with the now famous Hal 9000.

THE THOMAS CROWN AFFAIR
Mirisch-Simkoe-Solar, United Artists

- **Music (Song):** "The Windmills of Your Mind." Music by Michel Legrand. Lyrics by Alan and Marilyn Bergman.

This film, starring Faye Dunaway and Steve McQueen, is especially popular in France. McQueen's character was the "Raffles," or gentleman thief, of his era.

WINNIE THE POOH AND THE BLUSTERY DAY
Disney – Buena Vista

- **Short Subject (Cartoon):** Walt Disney, producer

The whole cast celebrates Christopher Robin's birthday!

ROBERT KENNEDY REMEMBERED
Guggenheim Productions, National General

- **Short Subject (Live Action Subject):** Charles Guggenheim, producer

WHY MAN CREATES
Saul Bass and Associates

- **Documentary (Short Subject):** Saul Bass, producer

JOURNEY INTO SELF
Western Behavioral Sciences Institute

- **Documentary (Feature):** Bill McGraw, producer

WAR AND PEACE
Russia

- **Foreign Language Film**

PLANET OF THE APES
Apjac, 20ᵗʰ Century-Fox

- **Honorary Award:** John Chambers, for outstanding make-up achievement

An ape guards prisoner Charlton Heston, who is soon to be made into a slave.

This Russian film was the definitive movie of Leo Tolstoy's novel.

1969

MIDNIGHT COWBOY
Hellman-Schlesinger, United Artists

- **Best Picture:** Produced by Jerome Hellman
- **Direction:** John Schlesinger
- **Writing (Screenplay based on material from another medium):** Waldo Salt

TRUE GRIT
Wallis, Paramount

- **Best Actor:** John Wayne

John Wayne used Kim Darby's shoulder to sight and shoot, as his health and eyesight fail him.

Cowboy Jon Voight is helped by Dustin Hoffman (Ratso Rizzo) in N.Y.C.

THE PRIME OF MISS JEAN BRODIE
20ᵗʰ Century-Fox

- **Best Actress:** Maggie Smith

Maggie Smith teaches her "Brodie" girls in Edinburgh.

They Shoot Horses, Don't They?
Chartoff-Winkler-Pollack, ABC Pictures, Cinerama

- **Best Supporting Actor:** Gig Young

Depression era dance marathon emcee Gig Young leads the band and the event.

Cactus Flower
Frankovitch, Columbia

- **Best Supporting Actress:** Goldie Hawn

Left to right: Walter Matthau, Goldie Hawn, Jack Weston, and Ingrid Bergman share a night out.

Butch Cassidy and the Sundance Kid
Hill-Monash, 20th Century-Fox

- **Writing (Story and Screenplay based on material not previously published or produced):** William Goldman
- **Cinematography:** Conrad Hall
- **Music (Song):** "Raindrops Keep Fallin' on my Head." Music by Burt Bacharach. Lyrics by Hal David.
- **Music (Original Score for a motion picture [not a musical]):** Burt Bacharach

A light and happy moment early in the film, when Paul Newman (as Butch Cassidy) takes Katharine Ross for a bicycle ride at their hideout.

HELLO DOLLY!
Chenault, 20th Century-Fox

- **Art Direction–Set Decoration:** John DeCuir, Jack Martin Smith and Herman Blumenthal; Walter M. Scott, George Hopkins and Raphael Bretton
- **Sound:** Jack Solomon and Murray Spivack
- **Music (Score of a Musical Picture [original or adaptation]):** Lennie Hayton and Lionel Newman

Louis Armstrong and Barbra Streisand join forces in music.

ANNE OF THE THOUSAND DAYS
Wallis, Universal

- **Costume Design:** Margaret Furse

Richard Burton (King Henry VIII) confers with Genevieve Bujold (Anne Boleyn) in this historical drama.

Z
Reggane Films – O.N.C.I.C., Cinema V (Algerian)

- **Film Editing:** Francoise Bonnot
- **Foreign Language Film**

Yves Montand, center, is assassinated in this political thriller.

MAROONED
Frankovich-Sturges, Columbia

- **Special • Visual Effects:** Robbie Robertson

Gene Hackman (top), James Franciscus (on bicycle), and Richard Crenna (right), are three astronauts who are marooned in space.

IT'S TOUGH TO BE A BIRD
Disney, Buena Vista

- **Short Subject (Cartoon):** Ward Kimball, producer

THE MAGIC MACHINE
Fly-By-Night Productions, Manson Distributing

- **Short Subject (Live Action Subject):** Joan Keller Stern, producer

CZECHOSLOVAKIA
Sanders–Fresco Film Makers for U.S. Information Agency

- **Documentary (Short Subject):** Denis Sanders and Robert M. Fresco, producers

ARTHUR RUBINSTEIN – THE LOVE OF LIFE
Midem Productions

- **Documentary (Feature):** Bernard Chevry, producer

1970

PATTON
20th Century-Fox

- **Best Picture:** Produced by Frank Mc Carthy
- **Best Actor:** George C. Scott
- **Direction:** Franklin J. Schaffner
- **Writing (Story and Screenplay based on factual material or material not previously published or produced):** Francis Ford Coppola and Edmund H. North
- **Art Direction–Set Decoration:** Urie McCleary and Gil Parrondo, Antonio Mateos and Pierre-Louis Thevenet
- **Sound:** Douglas Williams and Don Bassman
- **Film Editing:** Hugh S. Fowler

George C. Scott (as Patton) is firmly in command.

WOMEN IN LOVE
Kramer-Rosen, United Artists

- **Best Actress:** Glenda Jackson

Glenda Jackson and Oliver Reed in a reflective moment.

RYAN'S DAUGHTER
Faraway, M-G-M

- **Best Supporting Actor:** John Mills
- **Cinematography:** Freddie Young

With the west coast of Ireland as the setting, Sarah Miles patiently waits for Trevor Howard and John Mills (as the village idiot) to return her parasol.

AIRPORT
Hunter, Universal

- **Best Supporting Actress:** Helen Hayes

Helen Hayes is a stowaway caught by Jacqueline Bisset, and introduced to pilot Dean Martin. This was Hayes's first film in 14 years. She became the first actress to win both Best Actress and Best Supporting Actress over the years.

CROMWELL
Irving Allen, Columbia

- **Costume Design:** Nino Novarese

Richard Harris (as Cromwell) argues with Alec Guinness (King Charles I), while Dorothy Tutin observes.

M*A*S*H
Aspen, 20th Century-Fox

- **Writing (Screenplay based on material from another medium):** Ring Lardner, Jr.

Donald Sutherland and Elliot Gould play two doctors trying to have some fun as a relief from caring for the wounded and dying in the Korean War.

TORA! TORA! TORA!
20th Century-Fox

- **Special Visual Effects:** A.D. Flowers and L.B. Abbott

This Spanish one-sheet poster shows the many stars of this film. American lobby cards and posters tend to be more artistic.

LOVERS AND OTHER STRANGERS
ABC Pictures, Cinerama

- **Music (Song):** "For All We Know." Music by Fred Karlin. Lyrics by Robb Royer and James Griffin (aka Robb Wilson and Arthur James)

Bonnie Bedelia and Michael Brandon get married in this comedy.

LOVE STORY
Paramount

- **Music (Original Score):** Francis Lai

Ali MacGraw and Ryan O'Neal never have to say they are sorry for their performances in this film!

LET IT BE
Beatles-Apple Productions, United Artists

- **Musical (Original Song Score):** The Beatles

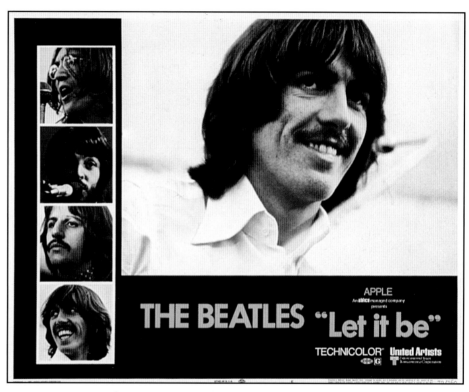

Beatles documentary starring, top to bottom, John Lennon, Paul McCartney, Ringo Starr, and George Harrison.

Is it Always Right to be Right?
Stephen Bosustow Productions, Schoenfeld Films

- Short Subject (Cartoon): Nick Bosustow

The Resurrection of Broncho Billy
University of Southern California, Department of Cinema, Universal

- **Short Subject (Live Action Subject):** John Longenecker, producer

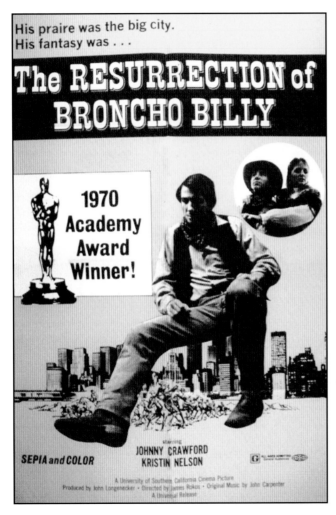

Johnny Crawford and Kristin Nelson star in this short.

Interviews With My Lai Veterans
Laser Film

- **Documentary (Short Subject):** Joseph Strick producer

Woodstock
Wadleigh-Maurice, Warner Brothers

- **Documentary (Feature):** Bob Maurice, producer

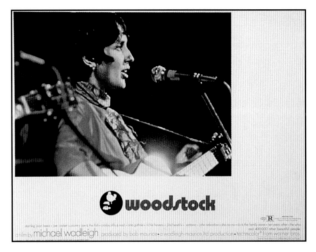

Joan Baez is one of the great talents who performed at the famous Woodstock outdoor rock concert and festival of love.

Investigation of a Citizen Above Suspicion
Italy

- **Foreign Language Film**

A murder film about a police chief who wants to be captured for his foul deeds.

1971

THE FRENCH CONNECTION
D'Antoni-Schine-Moore, 20th Century-Fox

- **Best Picture:** Produced by Philip D'Antoni
- **Best Actor:** Gene Hackman
- **Direction:** William Friedkin
- **Writing (Screenplay based on material from another medium):** Ernest Tidyman
- **Film Editing:** Jerry Greenberg

Gene Hackman, as detective "Popeye" Doyle, kills a hitman (Michael Bozzuffi) after a fantastic car/train chase.

KLUTE
Gus, Warner Brothers

- **Best Actress:** Jane Fonda

Jane Fonda (as Bree) and Donald Sutherland (as Detective Klute) work together to trap Fonda's stalker.

THE LAST PICTURE SHOW
BBS Productions, Columbia

- **Best Supporting Actor:** Ben Johnson
- **Best Supporting Actress:** Cloris Leachman

This re-release half-sheet (22" x 28") shows the cast plus Academy Award® winners. Top to bottom are Cybill Shepherd, Timothy Bottoms, Jeff Bridges, Ben Johnson, and Cloris Leachman.

197

THE HOSPITAL
Gottfried-Chayesfsky-Hiller, United Artists

- **Writing (Story and Screenplay based on factual material or material not previously published or produced):** Paddy Chayefsky

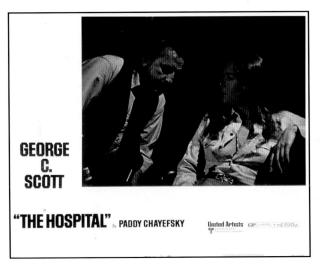

Aging, unhappy doctor George C. Scott and sultry mental patient Diana Rigg find quick affection in the hospital.

NICHOLAS AND ALEXANDRA
Horizon, Columbia

- **Art Direction–Set Decoration:** John Box, Ernest Archer, Jack Maxsted and Gil Parrando; Vernon Dixon
- **Costume Design:** Yvonne Blake and Antonio Castillo

Michael Jayston (as Czar Nicholas) and Janet Suzman (as Alexandra) pose for family portrait before the revolution took both their realms and their lives.

FIDDLER ON THE ROOF
Mirisch-Cartier, United Artists

- **Sound:** Gordon K. McCallum and David Hildyard
- **Cinematography:** Oswald Morris
- **Music (Scoring: Adaptation and Original Song Score):** John Williams

Topol (Tevye the milkman) sings "Sunrise, Sunset."

THE CRUNCH BIRD
Maxwell-Petok-Petrovich Productions, Regency Films

- **Short Subject (Animated Film):** Ted Petok, producer

SENTINELS OF SILENCE
Producciones Concord, Paramount

- **Short Subject (Live Action Film):** Manuel Arango and Robert Amram, producers
- **Documentary (Short Subject)**

BUTTERFLIES ARE FREE
Frankovich, Columbia

- **Best Supporting Actress:** Eileen Heckart

Eileen Heckert, Goldie Hawn, and Eddie Albert star in a blind boy's love for his wacky next door neighbor.

THE CANDIDATE
Redford – Ritchie, Warner Brothers

- **Writing (Story and Screenplay based on factual material or material not previously published or produced):** Jeremy Larner

Robert Redford, backed by bearded Peter Boyle, seeks to run an honest campaign in this political satire.

TRAVELS WITH MY AUNT
Fryer, M-G-M

- **Costume Design:** Anthony Powell

Maggie Smith travels in style around Europe.

A CHRISTMAS CAROL
American Broadcasting Company Film Services

- **Short Subject (Animated Film):** Richard Williams, producer

NORMAN ROCKWELL'S WORLD...AN AMERICAN DREAM
Concepts Unlimited, Columbia

- **Short Subject (Live Action Film):** Richard Barclay, producer

THIS TINY WORLD
A Charles Huguenot van der Linden Production

- **Documentary (Short Subject):** Charles and Martina Huguenot van der Linden, producers

MARJOE
Cinema X, Cinema 5, Ltd.

- **Documentary (Feature):** Howard Smith and Sarah Kernochan, producers

Marjoe Gortner, an evangelist who becomes an actor.

THE DISCREET CHARM OF THE BOURGEOISIE
France

- **Foreign Language Film**

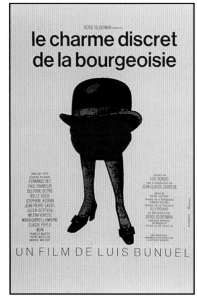

A surrealistic comedy starring Fernando Rey.

THE POSEIDON ADVENTURE
Irwin Allen, 20ᵗʰ Century-Fox

- **Music (Song):** "The Morning After." Music and lyrics by Al Kasha and Joel Hirschhorn.
- **Special Achievement Award:** Visual Effects, L.B. Abbott and A.D. Flowers

Most of this talented group escapes from an overturned ocean liner. Top to bottom, left to right: Jack Albertson, Arthur O'Connell, Shelley Winters, Red Buttons, Stella Stevens, Gene Hackman, Carol Lynley, Pamela Sue Martin, Roddy McDowall, and Ernest Borgnine.

LIMELIGHT
Charles Chaplin, Columbia

- **Music (Original Dramatic Score):** Charles Chaplin, Raymond Rasch, and Larry Russell

This film was made twenty years earlier, but only released in 1972. This scene shows a comedy sequence between Buster Keaton and Charles Chaplin.

1973

The Sting

Universal-Bill/Phillips-George Roy Hill Film Productions; Zanuck/Brown Presentation, Universal

- **Best Picture:** Tony Bill, Michael and Julia Phillips, producers
- **Direction:** George Roy Hill
- **Writing (Best Story and Screenplaybased on factual material or material not previously published or produced):** David S. Ward
- **Art Direction-Set Decoration:** Henry Bumstead; James Payne
- **Costume Design:** Edith Head
- **Film Editing:** William Reynolds
- **Music (Scoring–Original Song Score and/or Adaptation):** Marvin Hamlisch

...naw, top, does not trust scam artists Paul Newman and Robert Redford.

Save The Tiger

Filmways-Jalem-Cirandinha, Paramount

- **Best Actor:** Jack Lemmon

Jack Lemmon shines in an unhappy film.

A Touch Of Class

Brut, Avco Embassy

- **Best Actress:** Glenda Jackson

George Segal and Glenda Jackson star in a romantic comedy.

203

THE PAPER CHASE
Thompson-Paul, 20th Century-Fox

- **Best Supporting Actor:** John Houseman

Student Timothy Bottoms has trouble dealing with his demanding professor, John Houseman.

PAPER MOON
Directors Company, Paramount

- **Best Supporting Actress:** Tatum O'Neal

Ryan O'Neal watches headstrong real-life daughter Tatum O'Neal, as she tries to act way beyond her years.

THE EXORCIST
Hoya Productions, Warner Brothers

- **Writing (Best Screenplay based on material from another medium):** William Peter Blatty
- **Sound:** Robert Knudson and Chris Newman

Exorcist Max Von Sydow attempts to remove demonic spirits from a possessed Linda Blair.

CRIES AND WHISPERS
New World Pictures (Swedish)

- **Cinematography:** Sven Nykvist

Unforgettable Ingmar Bergman film starring Harriet Andersson, Liv Ullman, Ingrid Thulin, and Sven Nykvist.

MURDER ON THE ORIENT EXPRESS

G.W. Films, Paramount

- **Best Supporting Actress:** Ingrid Bergman

An Agatha Christie murder mystery, starring (left to right): George Coulouris, Anthony Perkins, Vanessa Redgrave, Sean Connery, Ingrid Bergman, Albert Finney (as Hercule Poirot), Wendy Hiller, Michael York, Rachel Roberts, Lauren Bacall, and Martin Balsam.

CHINATOWN

Robert Evans, Paramount

- **Writing (Original Screenplay):** Robert Towne

This international release lobby card shows Los Angeles private eye Jack Nicholson, hired by femme fatale Faye Dunaway, contemplating his next move.

THE TOWERING INFERNO

Irwin Allen, 20th Century-Fox / Warner Brothers

- **Cinematography:** Fred Koenekamp and Joseph Biroc
- **Film Editing:** Harold F. Kress and Carl Kress
- **Music (Song):** "We May Never Love Like This Again." Music and lyrics by Al Kasha and Joel Hirschhorn

Steve McQueen and Paul Newman head a cast for this gripping fire-fighting drama. Left to right in support are William Holden, Faye Dunaway, Fred Astaire, Susan Blakely, Richard Chamberlain, Jennifer Jones, O.J. Simpson, Robert Vaughn, and Robert Wagner.

THE GREAT GATSBY
David Merrick, Paramount

- **Costume Design:** Theoni V. Aldredge
- **Music (Scoring–Original Song Score and/or Adaptation):** Nelson Riddle

EARTHQUAKE
Robson-Filmakers Group, Universal

- **Sound:** Ronald Pierce and Melvin Metcalfe, Sr.
- **Special Achievement Awards – Visual Effects:** Frank Brendel, Glen Robinson, and Albert Whitlock

Robert Redford (Gatsby) enjoys a picnic with Mia Farrow.

Charlton Heston. Lloyd Nolan, and Ava Gardner do not look prepared for the forthcoming Los Angeles earthquakes.

CLOSED MONDAYS
Lighthouse Productions

- **Short Film (Animated Film):** Will Vinton and Bob Gardiner, producers

One-Eyed Men Are Kings
C.A.P.A.C. Productions (Paris)
- **Short Film (Live Action Film):** Paul Claudon and Edmond Sechan, producers

Don't
R.A. Films

- **Documentary (Short Subject):** Robin Lehman, producer

Hearts and Minds
Touchstone-Audjeff-BBS Production, Zuker/Jaglom-Rainbow Pictures

- **Documentary (Feature):** Peter Davis and Bert Schneider, producers

Amarcord
Italy

- **Foreign Language Film**

Federico Fellini's classic comedy set in prewar Italy, with a cast largely unknown to American viewers.

American heroes are being honored in this photo.

1975

One Flew Over the Cuckoo's Nest
Fantasy Films, United Artists

- **Best Picture:** Produced by Saul Zaentz and Michael Douglas
- **Best Actor:** Jack Nicholson
- **Best Actress:** Louise Fletcher
- **Direction:** Milos Forman
- **Writing (Screenplay adapted from other material):** Lawrence Hauben and Bo Goldman

Head nurse Louise Fletcher puts up with convict Jack Nicholson, as he tries to encourage fellow mental institution patients to assert themselves.

The Sunshine Boys
M-G-M

- **Best Supporting Actor:** George Burns

In this film, former vaudeville partners George Burns and Walter Matthau still argue, even after their many years together. Here, they disagree as they prepare for a television special.

Shampoo
Rubeeker, Columbia

- **Best Supporting Actress:** Lee Grant

Warren Beatty , a sexy and restless hairdresser, argues while Lee Grant awaits her hairdo.

DOG DAY AFTERNOON
Warner Brothers

- **Writing (Original Screenplay):** Frank Pierson

Al Pacino takes a hostage in what turns out to be an unsuccessful bank robbery.

BARRY LYNDON
Hawk Films, Warner Brothers

- **Cinematography:** John Alcott
- **Art Direction–Set Decoration:** Ken Adam and Roy Walker, Vernon Dixon
- **Costume Design:** Britt Soderlund and Milena Canonero
- **Music (Scoring–Original Song Score and/or Adaptation):** Leonard Rosenman

Ryan O'Neal and Marisa Berenson are wed in 18th century Ireland.

JAWS
Zanuck / Brown, Universal

- **Sound:** Robert L. Hoyt, Roger Heman, Earl Madery and John Carter
- **Film Editing:** Verna Fields
- **Music (Original Score):** John Williams

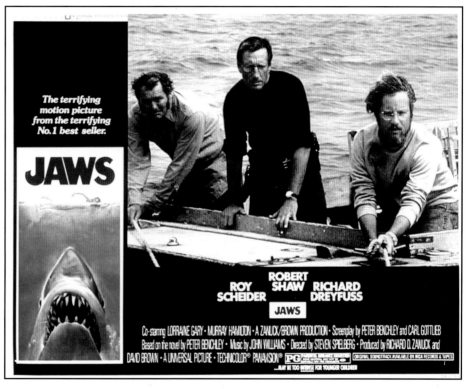

Robert Shaw, Roy Scheider, and Richard Dreyfuss attempt to catch the man-eating shark that terrorizes the east coast.

NASHVILLE
ABC – Weintraub – Altman, Paramount

- **Music (Song):** "I'm Easy." Music and lyrics by Keith Carradine

Keith Carradine sings to a talkative Nashville crowd.

GREAT
Grantstern, British Lion Films Ltd.

- **Short Film (Animated Film):** Bob Godfrey, producer

ANGEL AND BIG JOE
Salzman Productions

- **Short Film (Live Action):** Bert Salzman, producer

THE END OF THE GAME
Opus Films, Ltd.

- **Documentary (Short Subject):** Claire Wilbur and Robin Lehman, producers

THE MAN WHO SKIED DOWN EVEREST
Crawley Films

- **Documentary (Feature):** F.R. Crawley, James Hager and Dale Hartleben, producers

Skiing expedition of Japanese skier Yuichiro Miura.

Dersu Uzala
U.S.S.R.

- Foreign Language Film

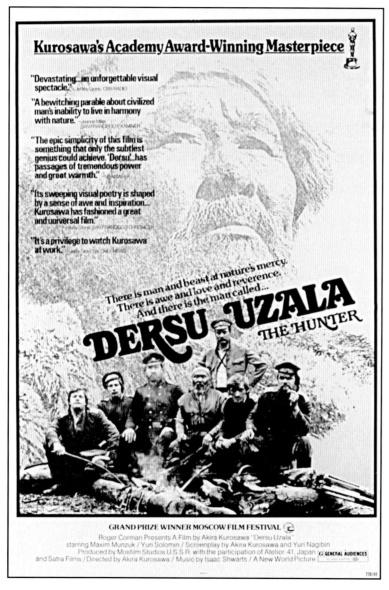

Russian film about exploring for gold in Siberia.

The Hindenburg
Robert Wise, Filmakers Group, Universal

- **Special Achievement Award:** Peter Berkos, Sound Effects
- **Special Achievement Award:** Albert Whitlock and Glen Robinson, Visual Effects

George C. Scott and Anne Bancroft are passengers on the ill-fated 1937 crash of the Hindenburg zeppelin.

1976

ROCKY
Chartoff-Winkler, United Artists

- **Best Picture:** Produced by Irwin Winkler and Robert Chartoff
- **Direction:** John G. Avildsen
- **Film Editing:** Richard Halsey and Scott Conrad

Sylvester Stallone (Rocky) and Carl Weathers (Apollo Creed) are friendly competitors.

NETWORK
Gottfried/Chayefsky, M-G-M, United Artists

- **Best Actor:** Peter Finch
- **Best Actress:** Faye Dunaway
- **Best Supporting Actress:** Beatrice Straight
- **Writing (Screenplay written directly for the screen):** Paddy Chayefsky

Peter Finch and Faye Dunaway work and play hard to increase ratings for their television station.

ALL THE PRESIDENT'S MEN
Wildwood, Warner Brothers

- **Best Supporting Actor:** Jason Robards
- **Writing (Screenplay based on material from another medium):** William Goldman
- **Art Direction–Set Decoration:** George Jenkins; George Gaines
- **Sound:** Arthur Piantadosi, Les Fresholtz, Dick Alexander and Jim Webb

Washington Post reporters investigate the Watergate cover-up. Left to right: Dustin Hoffman, Robert Redford, Jason Robards, Jack Warden, and Martin Balsam.

BOUND FOR GLORY
United Artists

- **Cinematography:** Haskell Wexler
- **Music (Original Song Score and Its Adaptation or Best Adaptation Score):** Leonard Rosenman

David Carradine (as folk singer Woody Guthrie) in a story set during the depression (1936-40).

FELLINI'S CASANOVA
Universal (Italian)

- **Costume Design:** Danilo Donati

Donald Sutherland, as Casanova, flirts with one of his many conquests.

A STAR IS BORN
Barwood/Peters-First Artists, Warner Brothers

- **Music (Song):** "Evergreen." Music by Barbra Streisand. Lyrics by Paul Williams

Kris Kristofferson and Barbra Streisand harmonize in a third rendition of this film.

THE OMEN
20th Century-Fox

- **Music (Original Score):** Jerry Goldsmith

David Warner and Gregory Peck in a story of the advent of the antichrist.

LEISURE
Film Australia

- **Short Film (Animated Film):** Suzanne Baker, producer

IN THE REGION OF ICE
American Film Institute

- **Short Film (Live Action):** Andre Guttfreund and Peter Werner, producers

NUMBER OUR DAYS
Community Television of Southern California

- **Documentary (Short Subject):** Lynne Littman, producer

HARLAN COUNTY, U.S.A.
Cabin Creek Films

- **Documentary (Feature):** Barbara Kopple, producer

Coal miners in Kentucky voicing their unhappiness about conditions.

BLACK AND WHITE IN COLOR
Ivory Coast

- **Foreign Language Film**

In an out-of-the-way African trading post at the beginning of World War I, French men, fueled by a surge of patriotism, decide to attack a German fort.

King Kong
DeLaurentiis, Paramount

- **Special Achievement Award for Visual Effects:** Carlo Rambaldi, Glen Robinson and Frank Van Der Veer

Logan's Run
Saul David, M-G-M

- **Special Achievement Award:** L.B. Abbott, Glen Robinson and Matthew Yuricich for Visual Effects

A fearsome image of the great Kong.

Jenny Agutter and Michael York fight those that seek to exterminate people thirty years of age and older.

ANNIE HALL
Rollins-Joffe, United Artists

- **Best Picture:** Produced by Charles H. Joffe
- **Best Actress:** Diane Keaton
- **Direction:** Woody Allen
- **Writing (Screenplay written directly for the screen):** Woody Allen and Marshall Brickman

THE GOODBYE GIRL
Stark, M-G-M / Warner Brothers

- **Best Actor:** Richard Dreyfuss

This bittersweet love story between amateur singer Diane Keaton and comic Woody Allen.

The characters portrayed by Richard Dreyfuss and Marsha Mason are forced by economics to share rooms in this comedy, and they fall in love in the process.

JULIA
20th Century-Fox

- **Best Actor:** Jason Robards
- **Best Supporting Actress:** Vanessa Redgrave
- **Writing (Screenplay based on material from another medium):** Alvin Sargent

CLOSE ENCOUNTERS OF THE THIRD KIND
Columbia

- **Cinematography:** Vilmos Zsigmond
- **Special Achievement Award:** Frank Warner, Sound Effects

Vanessa Redgrave and Jane Fonda are childhood chums who work together in the resistance.

Space visitors and humans make contact.

Jane Fonda (as author Lillian Hellman) and Jason Robards (as Dashiell Hammett) in this story of their interest in the 1930s Nazi resistance in Europe.

STAR WARS
20ᵗʰ Century-Fox

- **Art Direction–Set Decoration:** John Barry, Norman Reynolds and Leslie Dilley; Roger Christian
- **Costume Design:** John Mollo
- **Sound:** Don MacDougall, Roy West, Bob Minkler and Derek Ball
- **Film Editing:** Paul Hirsch, Marcia Lucas and Richard Chew
- **Visual Effects:** John Stears, John Dykstra, Richard Edlund, Grant McCune and Robert Blalack
- **Music (Original Score):** John Williams
- **Special Achievement Award:** Benjamin Burtt, Jr., Sound Effects

Mark Hamill, Carrie Fisher, and Harrison Ford battle "The Dark Side."

YOU LIGHT UP MY LIFE
Session Company, Columbia

- **Music:** "You Light up my Life." Music and lyrics by Joseph Brooks.

Didi Conn sings the title song, and acts the lead part of a young girl trying for success in the music world.

A LITTLE NIGHT MUSIC
Sascha – Wein / Elliot Kastner, New World Pictures

- **Music (Original Song Score and Its Adaptation or Best Adaptation Score):** Jonathan Tunick

This comedy/musical transferred from the stage to film.

Sand Castle
National Film Board of Canada

- **Short Film (Animated Film):** Co Hoedeman, producer

I'll Find a Way
National Film Board of Canada

- **Short Film (Live Action):** Beverly Shaffer and Yuki Yoshida, producers

Gravity is my Enemy
Joseph Production

- **Documentary (Short Subject):** John Joseph and Jan Stussy, producers

Who Are the Debolts? And Where Did They Get Nineteen Kids?
Korty Films / Charles M. Schultz, Sanrio Films

- **Documentary (Feature):** John Korty, Dan McCann and Warren L. Lockhart, producers

Madame Rosa
France

- **Foreign Language Film**

Simone Signoret, as Rosa, creates one of her finest roles as a former prostitute and concentration camp victim.

1978

THE DEER HUNTER

EMI / Cimino, Universal

- **Best Picture:** Produced by Barry Spikings, Michael Deeley, Michael Cimino and John Peverall
- **Best Supporting Actor:** Christopher Walken
- **Direction:** Michael Cimino
- **Sound:** Richard Portman, William McCaughey, Aaron Rochin, and Darin Knight
- **Film Editing:** Peter Zinner

Boyhood friends (clockwise) before the problems in Vietnam: Christopher Walken, John Cazale, George Dzundza, and Robert DeNiro.

COMING HOME

Hellman, United Artists

- **Best Actor:** Jon Voight
- **Best Actress:** Jane Fonda
- **Writing (Screenplay written directly for the screen):** Nancy Dowd, Waldo Salt and Robert C. Jones

Jane Fonda falls for paraplegic Jon Voight while her husband is in Vietnam.

CALIFORNIA SUITE

Stark, Columbia

- **Best Supporting Actress:** Maggie Smith

Maggie Smith and Michael Caine star in one of the four separate parts of this Neil Simon play.

MIDNIGHT EXPRESS
Casablanca, Columbia

- **Writing (Screenplay based on material from another medium):** Oliver Stone
- **Music (Original Score):** Giorgio Moroder

Brad Davis is shown in a Turkish prison, trying to figure a way to get out.

DAYS OF HEAVEN
OP, Paramount

- **Cinematography:** Nestor Almendros

Brooke Adams and Richard Gere harvest wheat in Texas.

HEAVEN CAN WAIT
Dogwood, Paramount

- **Art Direction–Set Decoration:** Paul Sylbert and Edwin O'Donovan; George Gaines

Prematurely deceased Warren Beatty returns to earth and is assisted by Julie Christie.

223

DEATH ON THE NILE
Brabourne-Goodwin, Paramount

- **Costume Design:** Anthony Powell

Another great Agatha Christie story, with another great cast: Simon Mac Corkindale, I.S. Johar, David Niven, Peter Ustinov, Jack Warden, Maggie Smith, and George Kennedy. Bottom row: Lois Chiles, Mia Farrow, Angela Lansbury, Bette Davis, and Olivia Hussey.

THANK GOD IT'S FRIDAY
Casablanca-Motown, Columbia

- **Music (Song):** "Last Dance." Music and lyrics by Paul Jabara.

Disco singer Donna Summer belts out the "Last Dance."

THE BUDDY HOLLY STORY
Innovisions – ECA, Columbia

- **Music (Original Song Score and Its Adaptation or Best Adaptation Score):** Joe Renzetti

Gary Busey convincingly sings and plays the role of the late great Buddy Holly.

SPECIAL DELIVERY
National Film Board of Canada

- **Short Film (Animated Film):** Eunice Macaulay and John Weldon, producers

TEENAGE FATHER
New Vision Inc. for the Chidren's Home Society of California

- **Short Film (Live Action):** Taylor Hackford, producer

THE FLIGHT OF THE GOSSAMER CONDOR
A Shedd Production

- **Documentary (Short Subject):** Jacqueline Phillips Shedd and Ben Shedd, producer

SCARED STRAIGHT
A Golden West Television Production

- **Documentary (Feature):** Arnold Shapiro, producer

GET OUT YOUR HANDKERCHIEFS
France

- **Foreign Language Film**

SUPERMAN
Dovemead Ltd. Productions, Alexander Salkind Presentation, Warner Brothers

- **Special Achievement Award:** Les Bowie, Colin Chilvers, Denys Coop, Roy Field, Derek Meddings and Zoran Perisic, for Visual Effects.

Margot Kidder and Christopher Reeve fly to safety and love.

Gerard Depardieu works hard to make his wife happy in bed.

1979

KRAMER VS. KRAMER
Jaffe, Columbia

- **Best Picture:** Produced by Stanley R. Jaffe
- **Best Actor:** Dustin Hoffman
- **Best Supporting Actress:** Meryl Streep
- **Direction:** Robert Benton
- **Writing (Screenplay based on material from another medium):** Robert Benton

Ex-spouses Dustin Hoffman and Meryl Streep battle for custody of their six year old son.

NORMA RAE
20th Century-Fox

- **Best Actress:** Sally Field
- **Music (Song):** "It Goes Like It Goes." Music by David Shire. Lyrics by Norman Gimbel.

Ron Leibman, center, has persuaded southerner Sally Field to unionize in New York City.

BEING THERE
Lorimar-Fernsehproduktion GmbH, United Artists

- **Best Supporting Actor:** Melvyn Douglas

Melvyn Douglas believes that his befuddled and simple gardener, Peter Sellers, is actually brilliant.

BREAKING AWAY
20th Century-Fox

- **Writing (Screenplay written directly for the screen):** Steve Tesich

The Cutters (Jackie Earle Haley, Daniel Stern, Dennis Christopher, and Dennis Quaid) win the big college bike race in a victory over the socially well-to-do yuppie team.

APOCALYPSE NOW
Omni Zoetrope, United Artists

- **Cinematography:** Vittorio Storaro
- **Sound:** Walter Murch, Mark Berger, Richard Beggs, and Nat Boxer

Choosing which lobby card to represent this movie was difficult because the principal players are not pictured together. Marlon Brando is unforgettable as Kurz, the former army officer.

ALIEN
20th Century-Fox

- **Visual Effects:** H.R. Giger, Carlo Rambaldi, Brian Johnson, Nick Allder and Denys Ayling

The entire cast, including the cat, are shown here before they are set upon, one by one, by a horrible creature. Left to right, they are: Harry Dean Stanton, Iam Holm, John Hurt, Veronica Cartwright, Tom Skerritt, Sigourney Weaver, and Yaphet Kotto.

ALL THAT JAZZ
20ᵗʰ Century-Fox

- **Art Direction–Set Decoration:** Philip Rosenberg and Tony Walton; Edward Stewart and Gary Brink
- **Costume Design:** Albert Wolsky
- **Film Editing:** Alan Heim
- **Music (Original Song and Score and Its Adaptation or Best Adaptation Score):** Ralph Burns

Roy Scheider, as choreographer Joe Gideon, teams up with Ben Vereen in a dance spectacular.

A LITTLE ROMANCE
Pan Arts, Orion

- **Music (Original Score):** Georges Delerue

Laurence Olivier plays a con man who watches out for young sweethearts Diane Lane and Thelonious Bernard.

EVERY CHILD
National Film Board of Canada

- **Short Film (Animated Film):** Derek Lamb, producer

BOARD AND CARE
Ron Ellis Films

- **Short Film (Live Action):** Sarah Pillsbury and Ron Ellis, producers

PAUL ROBESON: TRIBUTE TO AN ARTIST
Janus Films, Inc.

- **Documentary (Short Subject):** Saul J. Turrell, producer

A great portrait of Paul Robeson.

228

BEST BOY
Only Child Motion Pictures, Inc.

- **Documentary (Features)**: Ira Wohl, producer

This touching story is about Wohl's mentally challenged cousin's efforts to deal with the problems of everyday life.

THE TIN DRUM
Federal Republic of Germany

- **Foreign Language Film**

Spanish one-sheet poster showing David Bennet and his tin drum during the Nazi's reign in Germany.

THE BLACK STALLION
Omni Zoetrope, United Artists

- **Special Achievement Awards:** Sound Editing, Alan Splet

Mickey Rooney, Kelly Reno, and the Black Stallion may look disinterested here. There is, in fact, a lot of love between the three of them as they put their joint efforts into preparing for the championship race.

1980

ORDINARY PEOPLE
Wildwood, Paramount

- **Best Picture:** Produced by Ronald L. Schwary
- **Best Supporting Actor:** Timothy Hutton
- **Direction:** Robert Redford
- **Writing (Screenplay based on material from another medium):** Alvin Sargent

Parents Mary Tyler Moore and Donald Sutherland deal with the death of their son, and how it affects their remaining son, Timothy Hutton.

RAGING BULL
Chartoff-Winkler, United Artists

- **Best Actor:** Robert DeNiro
- **Film Editing:** Thelma Schoonmaker

Trainer Joe Pesci encourages Robert DeNiro (as fighter Jake La Motta).

COAL MINER'S DAUGHTER
Schwartz, Universal

- **Best Actress:** Sissy Spacek

This autobiography of Loretta Lynn stars Sissy Spacek in the title role, supported by Tommy Lee Jones as her husband.

MELVIN AND HOWARD
Linson/Phillips/Demme, Universal

- **Best Supporting Actress:** Mary Steenburgen
- **Writing (Screenplay written directly for the screen):** Bo Goldman

Mary Steenburgen (Lynda Drummer) and Paul LeMat (Melvin Drummer) believe themselves to be the heirs of Howard Hughes's fortune.

TESS
Renn-Burrill, Columbia

- **Cinematography:** Geoffrey Unsworth and Ghislain Cloquet
- **Art Direction–Set Decoration:** Pierre Guffroy and Jack Stephens
- **Costume Design:** Anthony Powell

Natassia Kinski (Tess) gains social acceptance, but has difficulty holding it. (French lobby card).

THE EMPIRE STRIKES BACK
Lucasfilm, 20th Century-Fox

- **Sound:** Bill Varney, Steve Maslow, Gregg Landaker, and Peter Sutton
- **Special Achievement Award:** Brian Johnson, Richard Edlund, Dennis Muren, and Bruce Nicholson for Visual Effects

C3PO and R2D2 are unlikely heroes in the second Star Wars adventure.

FAME
M-G-M

- **Music (Song):** "Fame." Music by Michael Gore. Lyrics by Dean Pitchford.

Broadway hopefuls seek fame.

THE FLY
Pannonia Film, Budapest

- **Short Film (Animated Film):** Ferenc Rofusz, producer

THE DOLLAR BOTTOM
Rocking Horse Films, Ltd., Paramount

- **Short Film (Live Action):** Lloyd Phillips, producer

KARL HESS: TOWARD LIBERTY
Halle / Ladue, Inc.

- **Documentary:** Roland Halle and Peter W. Ladue, producers

FROM MAO TO MOZART: ISSAC STERN IN CHINA
The Hopewell Foundation

- **Documentary (Feature):** Murray Lerner, producer

MOSCOW DOES NOT BELIEVE IN TEARS
U.S.S.R.

- **Foreign Language Film**

Vera Alentova and Natalya Vavilova in a Russian film that follows the adventures of three young girls in Moscow after World War II.

1981

CHARIOTS OF FIRE
Enigma, The Ladd Company / Warner Brothers

- **Best Picture:** Produced by David Puttnam
- **Writing (Screenplay based on material from another medium):** Colin Welland
- **Costume Design:** Milena Canonero
- **Music (Original Score):** Vangelis

Ben Cross and Ian Charlson in a school competition preparing for the 1924 Olympic Games.

ON GOLDEN POND
ITC / IPC, Universal

- **Best Actor:** Henry Fonda
- **Best Actress:** Katharine Hepburn
- **Writing (Screenplay based on material from another medium):** Ernest Thompson

Academy Award® winners Henry Fonda and Katharine Hepburn enjoy their retired years at a pond in Maine.

ARTHUR
Rollins, Joffe, Morra and Brezner, Orion

- **Best Supporting Actor:** John Gielgud
- **Music (Song):** "Arthur's Theme (Best That You Can Do)." Music and lyrics by Burt Bacharach, Carole Bayer Sager, Christopher Cross, and Peter Allen

Dudley Moore's lovingly sarcastic valet, John Gielgud, won the Oscar®, but Moore and Liza Minnelli were both outstanding in this highly amusing and touching film as well.

REDS

J.R.S., Paramount

- **Best Supporting Actress:** Maureen Stapleton
- **Direction:** Warren Beatty
- **Cinematography:** Vittorio Storaro

Once again the Academy Award® winner is not on a lobby card, but Jack Nicholson, Diane Keaton, and Warren Beatty appear here representing the film.

RAIDERS OF THE LOST ARK

Lucasfilm, Paramount

- **Art Direction–Set Decoraton:** Norman Reynolds and Leslie Dilley; Michael Ford
- **Sound:** Bill Varney, Steve Maslow, Gregg Landaker and Roy Charman
- **Film Editing:** Michael Kahn
- **Visual Effects:** Richard Edlund, Kit West, Bruce Nicholson and Joe Johnston
- **Special Achievement Award:** Ben Burtt and Richard L. Anderson, for Sound Effects Editing

Great shot of Harrison Ford stealing the jewel before all hell breaks loose.

AN AMERICAN WEREWOLF IN LONDON

Lycanthrope / Polygram, Universal

- **Makeup:** Rick Baker

When the full moon rises, David Naughton turns into a werewolf .

CRAC

Societe Radio – Canada

- **Short Film (Animated Film):** Frederic Back, producer

VIOLET

The American Film Institute

- **Short Film (Live Action):** Paul Kemp and Shelley Levinson, producers

CLOSE HARMONY

A Nobel Enterprise

- **Documentary (Short Subject):** Nigel Nobel, producer

GENOCIDE

Arnold Schwartzman Productions, Inc.

- **Documentary (Short Subject):** Arnold Schwartzman and Rabbi Marvin Hier, producers

MEPHISTO

Hungary

- **Foreign Language Film**

A German actor became a Nazi to gain popularity and promise in this film.

1982

GANDHI
Columbia

- **Best Picture:** Produced by Richard Attenborough
- **Best Actor:** Ben Kingsley
- **Direction:** Richard Attenborough
- **Writing (Screenplay written directly for the screen):** John Briley
- **Cinematography:** Billy Williams and Ronnie Taylor
- **Art Direction–Set Decoration:** Stuart Craig and Bob Laing; Michael Seirton
- **Costume Design:** John Mollo and Bhanu Athaiya
- **Film Editing:** John Bloom

Ben Kingsley (as Gandhi) is visited in jail.

SOPHIE'S CHOICE
ITC / Pakula-Barish, Universal / A.F.D.

- **Best Actress:** Meryl Streep

Meryl Streep (as Sophie), hides her dark secrets from her lover, Kevin Kline.

AN OFFICER AND A GENTLEMAN
Lorimar / Elfland, Paramount

- **Best Supporting Actor:** Louis Gossett, Jr.
- **Music (Song):** "Up Where We Belong." Music by Jack Nitzsche and Buffy Sainte-Marie. Lyrics by Will Jennings.

Richard Gere (second from left) endures the verbal onslaught of Louis Gossett, Jr. in Naval Officer Candidate School.

235

TOOTSIE
Mirage / Punch, Columbia

- **Best Supporting Actress:** Jessica Lange

Jessica Lange exchanges girl-talk with Dustin Hoffman, dressed as Tootsie.

MISSING
Lewis, Universal

- **Writing (Screenplay based on material from another medium):** Costas-Gavras and Donald Stewart

Sissy Spacek and Jack Lemmon, as the relatives of a missing journalist in South America.

E.T. THE EXTRA – TERRESTRIAL
Universal

- **Sound:** Robert Knudson, Robert Glass, Don Digirolamo, and Gene Cantamessa
- **Visual Effects:** Carlo Rambaldi, Dennis Muren and Kenneth F. Smith
- **Sound Effects:** Charles L. Campbell and Ben Burtt
- **Music (Original Score):** John Williams

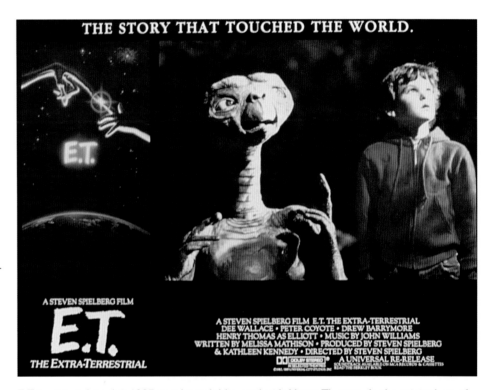

E.T. is pictured on this 1985 re-release lobby card with Henry Thomas. In the original set of lobbies, E.T. was not pictured in order to keep him as a surprise until the movie was viewed.

Victor / Victoria
M-G-M / United Artists

- **Music (Original Song Score and Its Adaptation or Best Adaptation Score):** Henry Mancini and Leslie Bricusse

James Garner , Julie Andrews, and Robert Preston star in a delightful comedy.

Quest For Fire
ICC, 20ᵗʰ Century-Fox

- **Makeup:** Sarah Monzani and Michele Burke

Rae Dawn Chong and Everett McGill seek the knowledge to make fire.

Tango
Film Polski

- **Short Film (Animated Film):** Zbigniew Rybczynski, producer

A Shocking Accident
Flamingo Pictures, Ltd.

- **Short Film (Live Action):** Christine Oestreicher, producer

If You Love This Planet
National Film Board of Canada

- **Documentary (Short Subject):** Edward Le Lorrain and Terri Nash, producers

Just Another Missing Kid
Canadian Broadcasting Corporation

- **Documentary (Feature):** John Zaritsky, producer

Volver A Empezar
Spain

- **Foreign Language Film**

1983

TERMS OF ENDEARMENT
Brooks, Paramount

- **Best Picture:** Produced by James L. Brooks
- **Best Actress:** Shirley MacLaine
- **Best Supporting Actor:** Jack Nicholson
- **Direction:** James L. Brooks
- **Writing (Screenplay based on material from another medium):** James L. Brooks

Shirley MacLaine, Debra Winger, and Jack Nicholson star in this multiple Academy Award® winner.

TENDER MERCIES
EMI, Universal / AFD

- **Best Actor:** Robert Duvall
- **Writing (Screenplay written directly for the screen):** Horton Foote

Robert Duvall on the country music comeback trail!

THE YEAR OF LIVING DANGEROUSLY
Fields, M-G-M / United Artists

- **Best Supporting Actress:** Linda Hunt

Academy Award® winner Linda Hunt perches on the shoulder of Mel Gibson. (Spanish lobby card)

FANNY AND ALEXANDER
Embassy

- **Cinematography:** Sven Nykvist
- **Art Direction–Set Decoration:** Anna Asp
- **Costume Design:** Marik Vos
- **Foreign Language Film** (Sweden)

Pernilla Allwin and Bertil Guve are the stars of this turn-of-the-century Ingmar Bergman classic.

THE RIGHT STUFF
Chartoff-Winkler. The Ladd Company through Warner Brothers

- **Sound:** Mark Berger, Tom Scott, Randy Thom and David MacMillan
- **Film Editing:** Glenn Farr, Lisa Fruchtman, Stephen A. Rotter, Douglas Stewart and Tom Rolf
- **Sound Effects Editing:** Jay Boekelheide
- **Music (Original Score):** Bill Conti

Left to right: Fred Ward, Dennis Quaid, Scott Paulin, Ed Harris, Charles Franik, Scott Glenn, and and Lance Henriksen. They all clearly have the right stuff!

FLASHDANCE
Polygram, Paramount

- **Music (Song):** "Flashdance…What a Feeling." Music by Giorgio Moroder. Lyrics by Keith Forsey and Irene Cara

Jennifer Beals struggles to achieve recognition for her dancing, and the fame which goes with it.

YENTL
Ladbroke / Barwood, M-G-M / United Artists

- **Music (Original Song Score and Its Adaptation or Best Adaptation Score):** Michel Legrand, Alan and Marilyn Bergman

Barbra Streisand lends her musical genius to the score of this movie, in which she assumed the persona of a man in order to be educated along with the Orthodox Jews.

SUNDAE IN NEW YORK
Motionpicker Production

- **Short Film (Animated Film):** Jimmy Picker, producer

BOYS AND GIRLS
Atlantis Films Ltd. Production

- **Short Film (Live Action):** Janice L. Platt, producer

FLAMENCO AT 5:15
National Film Board of Canada Production

- **Documentary (Short Subject):** Cynthia Scott and Adam Symansky, producers

HE MAKES ME FEEL LIKE DANCIN'
Edgar J. Scherick Associates Production

- **Documentary (Feature):** Emile Andolino, producer

RETURN OF THE JEDI
Lucasfilm, 20th Century-Fox

- **Special Achievement Award:** Richard Edlund, Dennis Muren, Ken Ralston and Phil Tippett for Visual Effects

Chewbacca, Carrie Fisher (Princess Leia), C-3PO, Mark Hamill (Luke Skywalker), and Harrison Ford (Han Solo) escape.

1984

AMADEUS
Zaentz, Orion

- **Best Picture:** Produced by Saul Zaentz
- **Best Actor:** F. Murray Abraham
- **Direction:** Milos Forman
- **Writing (Screenplay based on material from another medium):** Peter Schaffer
- **Art Direction–Set Decoration:** Patrizia Von Brandenstein; Karel Cerny
- **Costume Design:** Theodor Pistek
- **Sound:** Mark Berger, Tom Scott, Todd Boekelheide and Chris Newman
- **Makeup:** Paul LeBlanc and Dick Smith

AMADEUS

In the court of Emperor Joseph II, composer F. Murray Abraham (Antonio Salieri) is threatened by the talent of Tom Hulce (Mozart), who is shown here seeking help.

PLACES IN THE HEART
Tri-Star

- **Best Actress:** Sally Field
- **Writing (Screenplay written directly for the screen):** Robert Benton

Sally Field plays a Texas widow who fights to keep her home.

THE KILLING FIELDS
Enigma, Warner Brothers

- **Best Supporting Actor:** Haing S. Ngor
- **Cinematography:** Chris Menges
- **Film Editing:** Jim Clark

Haing S. Ngor, a Cambodian guide, helps New York Times journalist Sam Waterston.

A Passage to India
G.W. Films, Columbia

- **Best Supporting Actress:** Peggy Ashcroft
- **Music (Original Score):** Maurice Jarre

Peggy Ashcroft (Mrs. Moore) greets Indian women during her travels in the 1920s.

Indiana Jones and the Temple of Doom
Lucasfilm, Paramount

- **Visual Effects:** Dennis Muren, Michael McAlister, Lorne Peterson and George Gibbs

Kate Capshaw, Harrison Ford, and Ke Huy Quan always seem to be pursued by danger!

The Woman in Red
Orion

- **Music (Song):** "I Just Called to Say I Love You." Music and lyrics by Stevie Wonder

Kelly LeBrock (the woman in red) entrances the bumbling but loveable Gene Wilder in this comedy.

Purple Rain
Warner Brothers

- **Music (Original Song Score and Its Adaptation or Best Adaptation Score):** Prince

Great music, weak plot. The Artist Known as Prince stars.

CHARADE
Sheridan College Production

- **Short Film (Animated Film):** Jon Minnis, producer

UP
Pyramid Films

- **Short Film (Live Action):** Mike Hoover, producer

THE STONE CARVERS
Paul Wagner Producers

- **Documentary (Short Subjects):** Marjorie Hunt and Paul Wagner, producers

THE TIMES OF HARVEY MILK
Black Sand Education Productions, Inc.

- **Documentary:** Robert Epstein and Richard Schmiechen, producers

DANGEROUS MOVES
Switzerland

- **Foreign Language Film**

Michel Piccoli, Leslie Caron, Alexandre Arbatt, and Liv Ullman star in a story about the drama and intrigue of the International Chess Championship.

THE RIVER
Universal Pictures Production

- **Special Achievement Award:** Kay Rose, Sound Effects Editing

Harvey Milk was the first openly gay politician elected in San Francisco.

Sissy Spacek and Mel Gibson struggle to protect their farm from bank takeover and ruin.

243

1985

OUT OF AFRICA
Universal

- **Best Picture:** Produced by Sydney Pollack
- **Direction:** Sydney Pollack
- **Writing (Screenplay based on material from another medium):** Kurt Luedtke
- **Cinematography:** David Watkin
- **Art Direction–Set Decoration:** Stephen Grimes; Josie MacAvin
- **Sound:** Chris Jenkins, Gary Alexander, Larry Stensvold and Peter Handford
- **Music (Original Score):** John Barry

Robert Redford and Meryl Streep star in this beautiful love story in Nairobi, Africa.

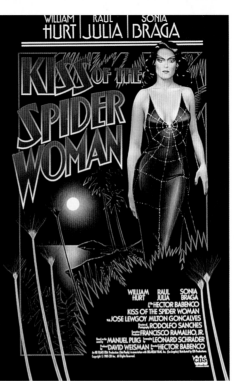

KISS OF THE SPIDER WOMAN
Island Alive

- **Best Actor:** William Hurt

William Hurt learned not to underestimate Sonia Braga , the Spider Woman!

THE TRIP TO BOUNTIFUL
Island

- **Best Actress:** Geraldine Page

Geraldine Page returns to happy times in a town called Bountiful.

COCOON
Zanuck-Brown, 20th Century-Fox

- **Best Supporting Actor:** Don Ameche
- **Visual Effects:** Ken Ralston, Ralph McQuarrie, Scott Farrar, and David Berry

PRIZZI'S HONOR
ABC, 20th Century-Fox

- **Best Supporting Actress:** Angelica Huston

Mafia black comedy film has Angelica Huston in love with hitman Jack Nicholson.

WITNESS
Feldman, Paramount

- **Writing (Screenplay written directly for the screen):** William Kelley, Pamela Wallace and Earl W. Wallace
- **Film Editing:** Thom Noble

Kelly McGillis, an Amish widow, attracts Harrison Ford, who is a policeman investigating a murder.

An awesome cast, including Wilford Brimley, Tahnee Welch, Maureen Stapleton, Brian Dennehy, Steve Guttenberg, Jack Gifford, Don Ameche, Hume Cronyn, Jessica Tandy, Ron Howard, and Gwen Verdon,

RAN
Orion Classics

- **Costume Design:** Emi Wada

Warlord Tatsuya Nakadai descends the stairs of his burning castle.

BACK TO THE FUTURE
Amblin, Universal

- **Sound Effects Editing:**
  Charles L. Campbell and
  Robert Rutledge

Christopher Lloyd and Michael
J. Fox are preparing to go
"back to the future!"

MASK
Universal

- **Makeup:** Michael Westmore
  and Zoltan Elek

Sam Elliott and Cher work
together to help their son
face a life disfigured by
disease.

WHITE NIGHTS
Columbia

- **Music (Song):** "Say You
  Say Me." Music and lyrics
  by Lionel Richie

Principal players are, left to
right, front: Isabella Rossellini,
Mikhail Baryshnikov (detective), and Jerzy Skolimowski
(KGB agent).

ANNA AND BELLA
The Netherlands

- **Short Film (Animated Film):** Cilia Van Dijk, producer

MOLLY'S PILGRIM
Phoenix Films

- **Short Film (Live Action Film):** Jeff Brown and Chris Pelzer, producers

WITNESS TO WAR: DR. CHARLIE CLEMENTS
Skylight Picture Production

- **Documentary (Short Subject):** David Goodman, producer

BROKEN RAINBOW
Earthworks Films Production

- **Documentary (Feature):** Maria Florio and Victoria Mudd, producers

THE OFFICIAL STORY
Argentina

- **Foreign Language Film**

Hector Alterio and Norma
Aleandro are concerned that
their adopted daughter's
parents were Argentinian
political prisoners.

1986

PLATOON
Hemdale, Orion

- **Best Picture:** Produced by Arnold Kopelson
- **Direction:** Oliver Stone
- **Sound:** John K. Wilkinson, Richard Rodgers, Charles "Bud" Grenzbach and Simon Kaye
- **Film Editing:** Claire Simpson

PLAT N

Tom Berenger and William Defoe are bitter enemies and competitors for leadership in this rugged Vietnam war film.

THE COLOR OF MONEY
Touchstone with Silver Screen Partners II, Buena Vista

- **Best Actor:** Paul Newman

Paul Newman, Tom Cruise, and Mary Elizabeth Mastrantonio hustle pool, as well as each other, in this sequel to "The Hustler."

CHILDREN OF A LESSER GOD
Sugarman, Paramount

- **Best Actress:** Marlee Matlin

Deaf janitor Marlee Matlin and teacher William Hurt show that love has a language all its own.

HANNAH AND HER SISTERS
Rollins and Joffe, Orion

- **Best Supporting Actor:** Michael Caine
- **Best Supporting Actress:** Dianne Wiest
- **Writing (Screenplay written directly for the screen):** Woody Allen

This film features Mia Farrow, Barbara Hershey, and Dianne Wiest as three sisters with varying interpersonal relationship issues.

A ROOM WITH A VIEW
Merchant Ivory, Cinecom

- **Writing (Screenplay based on material from another medium):** Ruth Prawer Jhabvala
- **Art Direction–Set Decoration:** Gianni, Quaranta and Brian Ackland-Snow; Brian Savegar and Elio Altramura
- **Costume Design:** Jenny Beaner and John Bright

Helena Bonham Carter and Julian Sands enjoy the view, and each other, in Florence, Italy.

THE MISSION
Warner Brothers

- **Cinematography:** Chris Menges

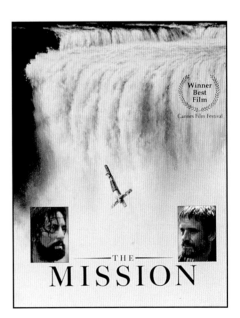

Robert DeNiro and Jeremy Irons as Jesuit missionaries in the Brazilian jungle. (Brochure).

ALIENS
20th Century-Fox

- **Sound Effects Editing:** Don Sharpe
- **Visual Effects:** Robert Skotak, Stan Winston, John Richardson and Suzanne Benson

Sigourney Weaver and her crew take on extraterrestrials.

'ROUND MIDNIGHT
Winkler, Warner Brothers

- **Music (Original Score):** Herbie Hancock

Jazz fan Francoise Cluzet shares a moment with saxophonist Dexter Gordon.

TOP GUN
Simpson / Bruckheimer, Paramount

- **Music (Song):** "Take My Breath Away." Music by Giorgio Moroder. Lyrics by Tom Whitlock.

Tom Cruise, as a fighter pilot in Top Gun training , falls in love with flight instructor Kelly McGillis. Val Kilmer (left) and Cruise compete to be the "Top Gun."

THE FLY
Brooksfilms, 20th Century-Fox

- **Makeup:** Chris Walas and Stephan Dupuis

Jeff Goldblum and Geena Davis at a happy time, before his experiment changes him into part man/part fly.

A Greek Tragedy
CineTe pvba

- **Short Film (Animated Film):** Linda Van Tulden and William Thijssen, producers

Precious Images
Calliope Films, Inc.

- **Short Film (Live Action):** Chuck Workman, producer

Women – For America, For the World
Educational Film and Video Project

- **Documentary (Short Subject):** Vivienne Verdon-Roe, producer

Artie Shaw: Time is All You've Got
Bridge Film Production

- **Documentary (Feature):** Brigitte Berman, producer

Artie Shaw, doing what he is known for!

Down and Out in America
Joseph Feury Production

- **Documentary (Feature):** Joseph Feury and Milton Justice, producers

The Assault
The Netherlands

- **Foreign Language Film**

Marc Van Uchelen stars as a boy who tries to forget his memories of the murder of his family at the end of World War II.

1987

THE LAST EMPEROR
Hemdale, Columbia

- **Best Picture:** Produced by Jeremy Thomas
- **Direction:** Bernardo Bertolucci
- **Writing (Screenplay based on material from another medium):** Mark Peploe and Bernardo Bertolucci
- **Cinematography:** Vittorio Storaro
- **Art Direction–Set Decoration:** Ferdinando Scarfiotti, Bruno Cesari and Osvaldo Desideri
- **Costume Design:** James Acheson
- **Sound:** Bill Rowe and Ivan Sharrock
- **Film Editing:** Gabriella Cristiani
- **Music (Original Score):** Ryuichi Sakamoto, David Byrne and Cong Su

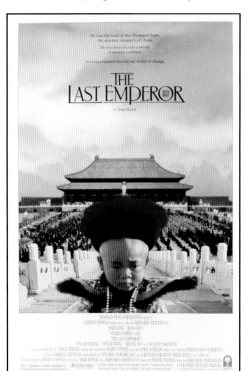

Epic film made in China, which won nine Academy Awards®, every single one for which it was nominated.

WALL STREET
Oaxatal, 20th Century-Fox

- **Best Actor:** Michael Douglas

Michael Douglas (left) as Gordon Gekko, and Charlie Sheen (as Bud Fox), interact in the sometimes shady world of high finance.

MOONSTRUCK
Palmer / Jewison, M-G-M

- **Best Actress:** Cher
- **Best Supporting Actress:** Olympia Dukakis
- **Writing (Screenplay written directly for the screen):** John Patrick Shanley

Olympia Dukakis and Cher, as mother and daughter, star in a story about warmth, love, and family in an Italian-American home.

251

THE UNTOUCHABLES
Linson, Paramount

- **Best Supporting Actor:** Sean Connery

Andy Garcia, Sean Connery, Kevin Costner (as Eliott Ness), and Charles Martin Smith fight Al Capone's crime machine during Prohibition in Chicago.

DIRTY DANCING
Vestron

- **Music (Song):** "(I've Had) the Time of my Life." Music by Franke Previte, John DeNicola and Donald Markowitz. Lyrics by Frank Previte.

Summer resort dancing instructor Patrick Swayze teaches sheltered vacationer Jennifer Grey more than dancing.

INNERSPACE
Warner Brothers

- **Visual Effects:** Dennis Muren, William George, Harley Jessup and Kenneth Smith

A Navy test pilot is experimentally shrunk, and then injected into the body of a hypochondriac, to combine comedy and science fiction in this film.

HARRY AND THE HENDERSONS
Amblin, Universal

- **Makeup:** Rick Baker

John Lithgow and Melinda Dillon bring home a hairy and unusual creature, assuming that it is dead. When it returns to life, they become deeply attached to it.

THE MAN WHO PLANTED TREES
Societe Radio-Canada / Canadian Broadcasting Corporation

- **Short Film (Animated Film):** Frederic Back, producer

RAY'S MALE HETEROSEXUAL DANCE HALL
Chanticleer Films

- **Short Film (Live Action):** Jonathan Sanger and Jana Sue Memel, producers

YOUNG AT HEART
Sue Marx Films, Inc. Production

- **Documentary:** Sue Marx and Pamela Conn, producers

THE TEN YEAR LUNCH: THE WIT AND LEGEND OF THE ALGONQUIN ROUND TABLE
Aviva Films Production

- **Documentary (Feature):** Aviva Slesin, producer

BABETTE'S FEAST
Denmark

- **Foreign Language Film**

Stephane Audrane stars as a Parisian, who finds refuge in a Danish village.

ROBOCOP
Tobor, Orion

- **Special Achievement Award:** Stephen Flick and John Pospisil, Sound Effects Editing

Reva Shwayder and Louis Gothelf seem young at heart.

Peter Weller stars as a mortally wounded police-man who is made into a futuristic crime-fighting cop.

1988

RAIN MAN
Guber-Peters, United Artists

- **Best Picture:** Produced by Mark Johnson
- **Best Actor:** Dustin Hoffman
- **Direction:** Barry Levinson
- **Writing (Screenplay written directly for the screen):** Screeenplay by Ronald Bass and Barry Morrow. Story by Barry Morrow.

Dustin Hoffman portrays the autistic Raymond, shown here taking a walk with his brother Charlie (Tom Cruise).

THE ACCUSED
Jaffe-Lansing, Paramount

- **Best Actress:** Jodie Foster

Is Jodie Foster lying as she accuses several men of gang-raping her? She is defended by District Attorney Kelly McGillis.

A FISH CALLED WANDA
Michael Shamberg-Prominent Features, M-G-M

- **Best Supporting Actor:** Kevin Kline

Jamie Lee Curtis, Michael Palin, and Kevin Kline plan a robbery, getaway, and division of loot. Note John Cleese in the border art for this comedy film.

THE ACCIDENTAL TOURIST
Warner Brothers

- **Best Supporting Actress:**
Geena Davis

Geena Davis, Kathleen Turner, and William Hurt star. Davis brings happiness to Hurt, who is estranged from wife Turner after the loss of their son.

MISSISSIPPI BURNING
Frederick Zollo, Orion

- **Cinematography:** Peter Biziou

FBI agents Gene Hackman and William Dafoe solve the case of three missing civil rights workers in Mississippi.

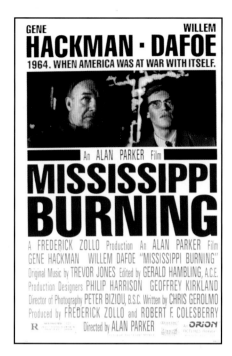

DANGEROUS LIAISONS
Warner Brothers

- **Writing (Screenplay based on material from another medium):**
Christopher Hampton
- **Art Direction–Set Decoration:**
Stuart Craig, Gerard James
- **Costume Design:** James Acheson

Glenn Close, John Malkovitch, and Michelle Pfeiffer compete for love and power in this intriguing tale.

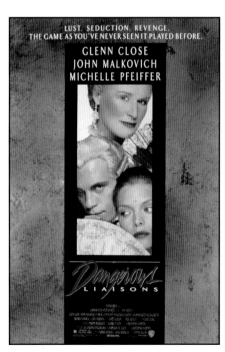

BIRD
Malpaso, Warner Brothers

- **Sound:** Les Fresholtz, Dick Alexander, Vern Poore and Willie D. Burton

Forrest Whitaker plays famed saxophonist Charlie Parker in this autobiographical film.

WHO FRAMED ROGER RABBIT?
Amblin Entertainment and Touchstone Pictures, Buena Vista

- **Film Editing:** Arthur Schmidt
- **Sound Effects Editing:** Charles L. Campbell and Louis L. Edemann
- **Visual Effects:** Ken Ralston, Richard Williams, Edward Jones and George Gibbs
- **Special Achievement Award:** Richard Williams, Animation Direction

Roger Rabbit is accused of murder, and is defended by Bob Hopkins in this innovative, part-animation comedy.

THE MILAGRO BEANFIELD WAR
Robert Redford / Moctesuma Esparza, Universal

- **Music (Original Score):** Dave Grusin

A film about laid-back life in Milagro, until something happens to change it.

WORKING GIRL
20th Century-Fox

- **Music (Song):** "Let the River Run." Music and lyrics by Carly Simon.

Melanie Griffith, Harrison Ford, and Sigourney Weaver star in this story of a secretary, a boss, and an old girl friend who won't let go.

BEETLEJUICE
Geffen / Warner Brothers

- **Makeup:** Steve LaPorte, Ve Neill, and Robert Short

It is obvious why this film won the makeup award! Michael Keaton (center) plays the title role of the spirit Betelgeuse.

TIN TOY
Pixar

- **Short Film (Animated):** John Lasseter and William Reeves, producers

THE APPOINTMENTS OF DENNIS JENNINGS
Schooner Productions, Inc.

- **Short Film (Live Action):** Dean Parisot and Steven Wright, producers

YOU DON'T HAVE TO DIE
Tiger Rose Productions in Association with Filmworks, Inc.

- **Documentary (Short Subject):** William Guttentag and Malcolm Clarke, producers

HOTEL TERMINUS: THE LIFE AND TIMES OF KLAUS BARBIE
The Memory Pictures Company

- **Documentary (Feature):** Marcel Ophuls, producer

Klaus Barbie (next to pillar) is seated behind his lawyer, Jacques Verges, at his trial in France.

PELLE THE CONQUEROR
Denmark

- **Foreign Language Film**

Widower Max Von Sydow and son Pelle Hvenegaard face hardships as 19th century immigrants to Denmark.

1989

DRIVING MISS DAISY
Zanuck Company, Warner Brothers

- **Best Picture:** Produced by Richard D. Zanuck and Lili Fini Zanuck
- **Best Actress:** Jessica Tandy
- **Writing (Screen play based on material from another medium):** Alfred Uhry
- **Makeup:** Manlio Rocchetti, Lynn Barber and Kevin Haney

Southern lady Jessica Tandy and her chauffeur, Morgan Freeman, find common ground.

MY LEFT FOOT
Ferndale / Grenada, Miramax

- **Best Actor:** Daniel Day-Lewis
- **Best Supporting Actress:** Brenda Fricker

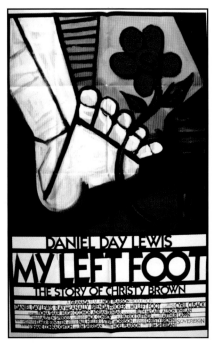

Daniel Day-Lewis and Brenda Fricker star in this Irish tale of a writer-artist with cerebral palsy.

GLORY
Tri-Star

- **Best Supporting Actor:** Denzel Washington
- **Cinematography:** Freddie Francis
- **Sound:** Donald O. Mitchell, Gregg C. Rudloff, Elliott Tyson and Russell Williams II

Andre Braugher, Morgan Freeman, Matthew Broderick, and Denzel Washington fight for the Union as America's first unit of Black soldiers.

BORN ON THE FOURTH OF JULY

A. Kitman Ho & Ixtlan, Universal

- **Direction:** Oliver Stone
- **Film Editing:** David Brenner and Joe Hutshing

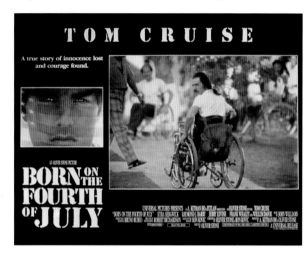

Tom Cruise plays Ron Kovic, an anti-war protester during the Vietnam War era.

DEAD POETS SOCIETY

Touchstone With Silver Screen Partners IV, Buena Vista

- **Writing (Screenplay written directly for the screen):** Tom Shulman

Robin Williams stars as a beloved prep school teacher whose influence over his students has some unexpected results. Note Ethan Hawke next to Williams.

BATMAN

Warner Brothers

- **Art Direction–Set Decoration:** Anton Furst; Peter Young

The Joker (Jack Nicholson) remains defiant, even in the face of Batman (Michael Keaton).

HENRY V
Renaissance Films with BBC, Samuel Goldwyn Company

- **Costume Design:** Phyllis Dalton

Kenneth Branagh leads his men at Agincourt.

INDIANA JONES AND THE LAST CRUSADE
Lucasfilm, Paramount

- **Sound Effects Editing:** Ben Burtt and Richard Hymns

Father and son, Sean Connery and Harrison Ford, fight Nazis while looking for the Holy Grail.

THE ABYSS
20th Century-Fox

- **Visual Effects:** John Bruno, Dennis Muren, Hoyt Yeatman, and Dennis Skotak

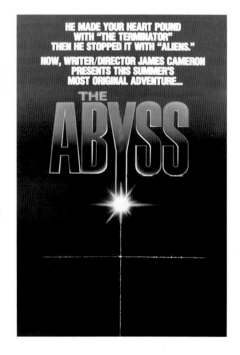

Underwater science fiction movie.

THE LITTLE MERMAID
Walt Disney Pictures with Silver Screen Partners IV, Buena Vista

- **Music (Song):** "Under the Sea." Music by Alan Menken. Lyrics by Howard Ashman
- **Music (Original Score):** Alan Menken

Ariel the mermaid wants to become human.

BALANCE
Lauenstein Production

- **Short Film (Animated Film):** Christopher Lauenstein and Wolfgang Lauenstein, producers

WORK EXPERIENCE
North Inch Production, Ltd.

- **Short Film (Live Action):** James Hendrie, producer

THE JOHNSTOWN FLOOD
Guggenheim Production Inc.

- **Documentary (Short Subject):** Charles Guggenheim, producer

COMMON THREADS: STORIES FROM THE QUILT
Telling Pictures and The Couturie Company Production

- **Documentary (Feature):** Robert Epstein and Bill Couturie, producers

CINEMA PARADISO
Italy

- **Foreign Language Film**

Projectionist Philippe Noiret and Salvatore Cascio, a boy fascinated with film, make a perfect pair.

1990

DANCES WITH WOLVES
Tig, Orion

- **Best Picture:** Produced by Jim Wilson and Kevin Costner
- **Direction:** Kevin Costner
- **Writing (Screenplay based on material from another medium):** Michael Blake
- **Cinematography:** Dean Semler
- **Sound:** Jeffrey Perkins, Bill W. Benton, Greg Watkins, and Russell Williams II
- **Film Editing:** Neil Travis
- **Music (Original Score):** John Barry

Kevin Costner, a Civil War veteran, makes his own personal peace with one of the leaders of the Lakota Sioux tribe.

REVERSAL OF FORTUNE
Reversal Films, Warner Brothers

- **Best Actor:** Jeremy Irons

Glenn Close (as Sunny Von Bulow), Jeremy Irons (as Claus Von Bulow), and Ron Silver (as attorney Alan Dershowitz) star in a film about attempted murder and the famous trial that follows.

MISERY
Castle Rock Entertainment, Columbia

- **Best Actress:** Kathy Bates

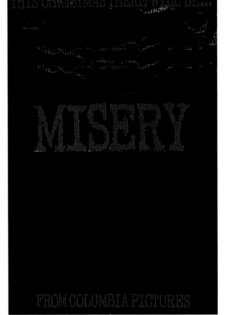

An advance poster for the movie based on a popular Stephen King book.

GOOD FELLAS
Warner Brothers

- **Best Supporting Actor:** Joe Pesci

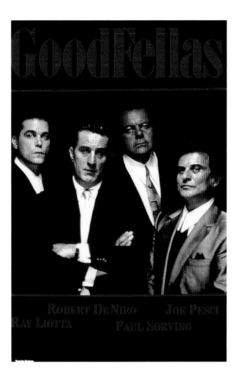

This is possibly the most popular movie poster of the 90s, showing the "Good Fellas": Ray Liotta, Robert DeNiro, Paul Sorvino, and Joe Pesci. (1998 re-release)

DICK TRACY
Touchstone Pictures, Buena Vista

- **Art Direction–Set Decoration:** Richard Sylbert; Rick Simpson
- **Music (Song):** "Sooner or Later (I Always Get my Man)." Music and lyrics by Stephen Sondheim.
- **Makeup:** John Caglione Jr. and Doug Drexler

The popular comic character comes to life in this film, featuring a cast including Warren Beatty and Madonna.

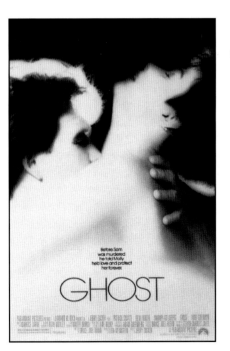

GHOST
Howard W. Koch, Paramount

- **Best Supporting Actress:** Whoopi Goldberg
- **Writing (Screenplay written directly for the screen):** Bruce Joel Rubin

Patrick Swayze and Demi Moore love each other, both before and after death.

CYRANO DE BERGERAC
Hachette Premiere / Camera One, Orion Classics

- **Costume Design:** Franca Squarciapino

Gerard Depardieu defends his honor and his nose.

THE HUNT FOR RED OCTOBER
Mace Neufeld / Jerry Sherlock, Paramount

- **Sound Effects Editing:** Cecilia Hall and George Watters, II

Sean Connery as a Russian nuclear submarine captain, who challenges Alec Baldwin, an American intelligence officer.

CREATURE COMFORTS
Aardman Animations Ltd. Production

- **Short Film (Animated):** Nick Park, producer

THE LUNCH DATE
Adam Davidson Production

- **Short Film (Live Action):** Adam Davidson, producer

DAYS OF WAITING
Mouchette Films Production

- **Documentary (Short Subject):** Steven Okazaki, producer

AMERICAN DREAM
Cabin Creek Films Production

- **Documentary (Feature):** Barbara Kopple and Arthur Cohn, producers

JOURNEY OF HOPE
Switzerland

- **Foreign Language Film**

Necmettin Cobanoglu, Emin Sivas, and Nur Surer are a Turkish family living in Switzerland.

TOTAL RECALL
Carolco Pictures Productions, Tri-Star

- **Special Achievement Award:** Erig Brevig, Rob Bottin, Tim McGovern and Alex Funke for Visual Effects.

Arnold Schwarzenegger flies to Mars in this futuristic 21st century thriller.

1991

THE SILENCE OF THE LAMBS
Strong Heart / Demme, Orion

- **Best Picture:** Produced by Edward Saxon, Kenneth Utt and Ron Bozman
- **Best Actor:** Anthony Hopkins
- **Best Actress:** Jodie Foster
- **Direction:** Jonathan Demme
- **Writing (Screenplay based on material previously produced or published):** Ted Tally

jodie foster · anthony hopkins · scott glenn

el silencio de los corderos
dirigida por jonathan demme

Anthony Hopkins (Hannibal Lecter) prepares for a meal! (Spanish lobby card)

CITY SLICKERS
Castle Rock Entertainment, Columbia

- **Best Supporting Actor:** Jack Palance

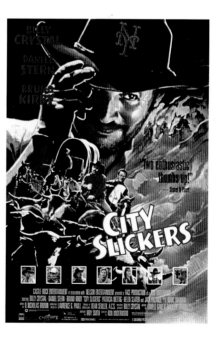

Jack Palance teaches Billy Crystal what the old west is really like. (Video poster)

the silence of the lambs

ORION

Scott Glenn, who is Jodie Foster's FBI boss, joins with her to capture a serial killer.

THE FISHER KING
Tri-Star

- **Best Supporting Actress:** Mercedes Ruehl

Mercedes Ruehl, Jeff Bridges, and Robin Williams contemplate Amanda Plummer's discovery.

THELMA AND LOUISE
Pathe Entertainment, M-G-M

- **Writing (Screenplay written directly for the screen):** Callie Khouri

Susan Sarandon and Geena Davis set out on a road trip adventure to escape their unhappy lives, only to ultimately face devastating consequences.

JFK
Camelot, Warner Brothers

- **Cinematography:** Robert Richardson
- **Film Editing:** Joe Hutshing and Pietro Scalia

Kevin Costner explains the FBI position concerning JFK's assassination.

BUGSY
Tri-Star

- **Art Direction–Set Decoration:** Dennis Gassner; Nancy Haigh
- **Costume Design:** Albert Wolsky

Annette Benning and Warren Beatty (as "Bugsy" Siegel) were couples on and off screen as well.

TERMINATOR 2: JUDGEMENT DAY
Carolco, Tri-Star

- **Sound Effects Editing:** Gary Rydstrom and Gloria S. Borders
- **Sound:** Tom Johnson, Gary Rydstrom, Gary Summers and Lee Orloff
- **Visual Effects:** Dennis Muren, Stan Winston, Gene Warren, Jr., and Robert Skotak
- **Makeup:** Stan Winston and Jeff Dawn

Arnold Schwarzenegger, a cyborg terminator, protects the world!

BEAUTY AND THE BEAST
Walt Disney Pictures, Buena Vista

- **Music (Song):** "Beauty and the Beast." Music by Alan Menken. Lyrics by Howard Ashman.
- **Music (Original Score):** Alan Menken

The beauty and the beast make beautiful music together.

MANIPULATION
Tandem Films Productoin

- **Short Film (Animated):** Daniel Greaves, producer

SESSION MAN
Chanticleer Films Production

- **Short Film (Live Action):** Seth Winston and Rob Fried, producers

DEADLY DECEPTION: GENERAL ELECTRIC, NUCLEAR WEAPONS AND OUR ENVIRONMENT
Women's Educational Media, Inc. Production

- **Documentary (Short Subject):** Debra Chasnoff, producer

IN THE SHADOW OF THE STARS
Light-Saraf Films Production

- **Documentary (Feature):** Allie Light and Irving Saraf, producers

MEDITERRANEO
Italy

- **Foreign Language Film**

Italian soldiers on a Greek Island in World War II fall in love with local girls like Vanna Barba.

1992

UNFORGIVEN
Warner Brothers

- **Best Picture:** Produced by Clint Eastwood
- **Best Supporting Actor:** Gene Hackman
- **Direction:** Clint Eastwood
- **Film Editing:** Joel Cox

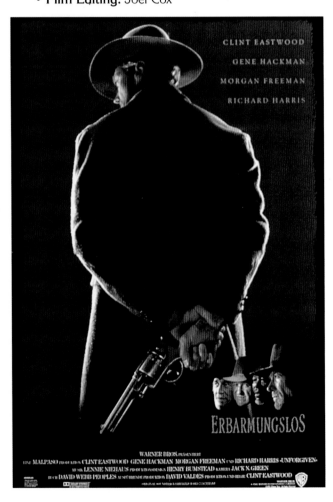

This poster image of Clint Eastwood has become a classic. Also featured: Richard Harris, Gene Hackman, and Morgan Freeman. (Spanish one-sheet)

SCENT OF A WOMAN
Universal Release / City Lights Films, Universal

- **Best Actor:** Al Pacino

Al Pacino defends Chris O'Donnell at his prep school.

HOWARD'S END
Merchant Ivory, Sony Pictures Classics

- **Best Actress:** Emma Thompson
- **Writing (Screenplay based on material prevously produced or published):** Ruth Prawer Jhabvala
- **Art Direction–Set Decoration:** Luciana Arrighi; Ian Whittaker

Lovers James Wilby and Helena Bonham Carter dominate this one-sheet poster. Shown at lower right are Emma Thompson, Anthony Hopkins and Vanessa Redgrave.

MY COUSIN VINNY
20th Century-Fox

- **Best Supporting Actress:** Marisa Tomei

Marisa Tomei and Joe Pesci light up the screen in this comedy.

A RIVER RUNS THROUGH IT
Columbia

- **Cinematography:** Philippe Rousselot

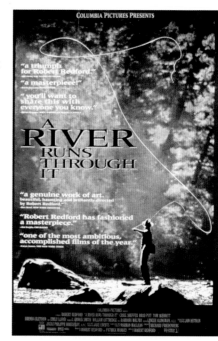

Breathtaking scenery and fly-fishing in Montana help a father to teach his sons about life.

THE CRYING GAME
Palace Pictures, Miramax

- **Writing (Screenplay written directly for the screen):** Neil Jordan

Jaye Davidson and Stephen Rea find forbidden love.

BRAM STOKER'S DRACULA
Columbia

- **Costume Design:** Eiko Ishioka
- **Sound Effects Editing:** Tom C. McCarthy and David E. Stone
- **Makeup:** Greg Cannom, Michele Burke and Matthew W. Mungle

Gary Oldman really takes a bite out of the role of Dracula!

THE LAST OF THE MOHICANS
20th Century-Fox

- **Sound:** Chris Jenkins, Doug Hemphill, Mark Smith, and Simon Kaye

Daniel Day-Lewis, as Hawkeye, is continually saving people throughout this film about the French and Indian War.

DEATH BECOMES HER
Universal

- **Visual Effects:** Ken Ralston, Doug Chiang, Doug Smythe, and Tom Woodruff Jr.

Border art shows Meryl Streep (with her head on backwards!), Bruce Willis, and Goldie Hawn, while Isabella Rossellini pricks Willis's finger in the large image at right.

ALADDIN
Walt Disney Pictures, Buena Vista

- **Music (Song):** "A Whole New World." Music by Alan Menken. Lyrics by Tom Rice.
- **Music (Original Score):** Alan Menken

This animated tale of the Arabian Nights is a musical delight.

MONA LISA DESCENDING A STAIRCASE
Joan C. Gratz Production

- **Short Film (Animated):** Joan C. Gratz, producer

OMNIBUS
Lazennec tout court / Le C.R.R.A.V. Production

- **Short Film (Live Action):** Sam Karmann, producer

EDUCATING PETER
State of the Art, Inc. Production

- **Documentary:** Thomas C. Goodwin and Geraldine Wurzburg, producers

THE PANAMA DECEPTION
Empowerment Project Production

- **Documentary (Feature):** Barbara Trent and David Kasper, producers

INDOCHINE
France

- **Foreign Language Film**

Peter Gwazdaukas, center, receives special help.

Catherine Deneuve stars in this film, which takes place in French Indochina.

271

1993

SCHINDLER'S LIST
Universal / Amblin, Universal

- **Best Picture:** Steven Spielberg, Gerald R. Molen and Branko Lustig, Producers
- **Direction:** Steven Spielberg
- **Writing (Screenplay based on material previously produced or published):** Steven Zaillian
- **Art Direction–Set Decoration:** Allan Starski; Ewa Braun
- **Cinematography:** Janusz Kaminski
- **Film Editing:** Michael Kahn
- **Music (Original Score):** John Williams

This multiple award winning film highlights Oscar Schindler (Liam Neeson) and his efforts to rescue Jews from the Nazi extermination camps.

PHILADELPHIA
Tri-Star

- **Best Actor:** Tom Hanks
- **Music (Song):** "Streets of Philadelphia." Music and lyrics by Bruce Springsteen

Tom Hanks, stricken with the AIDS virus, is helped by his lawyer, Denzel Washington, when his job is terminated as a result.

THE PIANO
Jan Chapman and CIBY 2000, Miramax

- **Best Actor:** Holly Hunter
- **Best Supporting Actress:** Anna Paquin
- **Writing (Screenplay written directly for the screen):** Jane Campion

Harvey Keitel and Holly Hunter become lovers in 19th century New Zealand.

THE FUGITIVE
Warner Brothers

- **Best Supporting Actor:** Tommy Lee Jones

U.S. Marshall Tommy Lee Jones on the trail of the fugitive.

MRS. DOUBTFIRE
20th Century-Fox

- **Makeup:** Greg Cannom, Ve Neill, Yolanda Toussieng

Pierce Brosnan and Robin Williams (as Mrs. Doubtfire) compete for the affection of Sally Fields and the children, Matthew Lawrence, Mara Wilson, and Lisa Jakub.

THE AGE OF INNOCENCE
Cappa / De Fina, Columbia

- **Costume Design:** Gabriella Pescucci

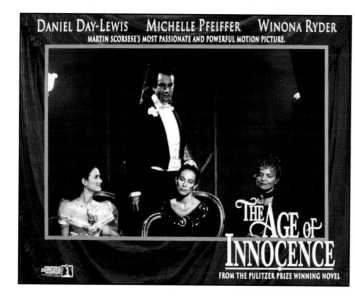

Winona Ryder, Daniel Day-Lewis, Geraldine Chaplin, and Michelle Pfeiffer at the theater in 1870 New York City.

JURASSIC PARK
Amblin, Universal

- **Sound:** Gary Summers, Gary Rydstrom, Shawn Murphy, and Ron Judkins
- **Sound Effects Editing:** Gary Rydstrom and Richard Hymns
- **Visual Effects:** Dennis Muren, Stan Winston, Phil Tippett, and Michael Lantieri

Jeff Goldblum, Richard Attenborough, Laura Dern, and Sam Neill with prehistoric dinosaur eggs.

I AM A PROMISE: THE CHILDREN OF STANTON ELEMENTARY SCHOOL
Verité Films Production

- **Documentary (Feature):** Susan and Alan Raymond, producers

These children, faces bright with promise, may well be the leaders of tomorrow.

DEFENDING OUR LIVES
Cambridge Documentary Films Production

- **Documentary (Short Subject):** Margaret Lazarus and Renner Wunderlich, producers

BELLE EPOQUE
Spain

- **Foreign Language Film**

Penelope Cruz falls in love with army deserter Jorge Sanz in Spain in 1931.

THE WRONG TROUSERS
Aardman Animations Ltd.

- **Short Film (Animated):** Nick Park, producer

A well-knit story starring Gromit.

BLACK RIDER (SCHWARZFAHRER)
Trans-Film GmbH Production

- **Short Film (Live Action):** Pepe Danquart, producer

1994

FORREST GUMP
Steve Tisch / Wendy Finerman, Paramount

- **Best Picture:** Wendy Finerman, Steve Tisch, and Steve Starkey, Producers
- **Best Actor:** Tom Hanks
- **Direction:** Robert Zemeckis
- **Writing (Screenplay based on material previously produced or published):** Eric Roth
- **Film Editing:** Arthur Schmidt
- **Visual Effects:** Ken Ralston, George Murphy, Stephen Rosenbaum, and Allen Hall

Gary Sinese, Mykelti Williamson, and Tom Hanks (as Forrest Gump) in this multiple Academy Award® winning film.

BLUE SKY

BLUE SKY
Robert H. Solo, Orion

- **Best Supporting Actress:** Jessica Lange

Jessica Lange greets Powers Boothe with a flirtatious look, and Carrie Snodgrass appears to be less than amused.

ED WOOD
Touchstone, Buena Vista

- **Best Supporting Actor:** Martin Landau
- **Makeup:** Rick Baker, Ve Neill, and Yolanda Toussieng

Johnny Depp and Martin Landau (as Bela Lugosi) strike Dracula-like poses.

BULLETS OVER BROADWAY
Jean Doumanian, Miramax

- **Best Supporting Actress:** Dianne Wiest

Dianne Wiest stars as a 1920s theatrical queen in this film, along with John Cusack and Jennifer Tilly.

PULP FICTION
A Band Apart / Jersey Films, Miramax

- **Writing (Screenplay written directly for the screen):** Screenplay by Quentin Tarantino. Stories by Quentin Tarantino and Roger Avary.

John Travolta and Samuel L. Jackson as professional hitmen.

LEGENDS OF THE FALL
Tri-Star

- **Cinematography:** John Toll

Aidan Quinn, Anthony Hopkins, Henry Thomas, and Brad Pitt star in a story about three brothers who compete for love, respect, and eventual control of their Montana Ranch.

THE MADNESS OF KING GEORGE
Close Call Films, Goldwyn/Channel Four

- **Art Direction–Set Decoration:** Ken Adam and Carolyn Scott

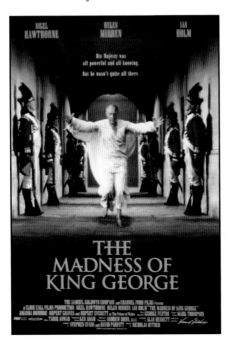

Nigel Hawthorne plays King George III, whose dementia affects his ability to rule wisely.

THE ADVENTURES OF PRISCILLA, QUEEN OF THE DESERT
Latent Images, Gramercy

- **Costume Design:** Lizzy Gardiner and Tim Chappel

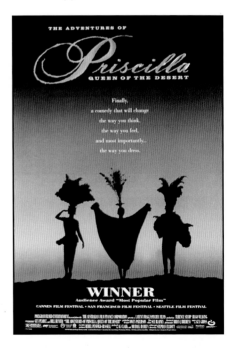

The outrageous exploits of two drag queens and a transsexual as they travel through small towns en route to their gigs.

THE LION KING
Disney, Buena Vista

- **Music (Song):** "Can You Feel the Love Tonight?." Music by Elton John. Lyrics by Tim Rice.
- **Music (Original Score):** Hans Zimmer

The majestic lion surveys his domain.

SPEED
20ᵗʰ Century-Fox

- **Sound:** Gregg Landaker, Steve Maslow, Bob Beemer, David R.B. MacMillan
- **Sound Effects Editing:** Stephen Hunter Flick

Keanu Reeves saves a busload of people in this intensely suspenseful and exciting film. (Flyer)

MAYA LIN: A STRONG CLEAR VISION
American Film Foundation / Sanders and Mock Productions

- **Documentary (Feature):** Freida Lee Mock and Terry Sanders, producers

An on-scene interview with Maya Lin and Freida Lee Mock

A TIME FOR JUSTICE
Guggenheim Productions, Inc., Production for the Southern Poverty Law Center

- **Documentary (Short Subject):** Charles Guggenheim, producer

BURNT BY THE SUN
Russia

- **Foreign Language Film**

Nikita Mikhalkova, Nadezhda Mikhalkova and Ingeborga Dapkunaite comprise a family in Russia that is confronted by Stalinism in 1936.

BOB'S BIRTHDAY
Snowdon Fine Animation for Channel Four / National Film Board of Canada Production

- **Short Film (Animated):** Alison Snowdon and David Fine, producers

FRANZ KAFKA'S IT'S A WONDERFUL LIFE
Conundrum Films Production

- **Short Film (Live Action):** Peter Capaldi and Ruth Kenley-Letts, producers

Richard E. Grant in a dramatic and expressive scene from this short.

TREVOR
Rajski / Stone Production

- **Short Film (Live Action):** Peggy Rajski and Randy Stone, producers

Brett Barsky starts in this film short.

1995

BRAVEHEART
Icon / Ladd Company, Paramount

- **Best Picture:** Mel Gibson, Alan Ladd Jr., and Bruce Davey, Producers
- **Direction:** Mel Gibson
- **Cinematography:** John Toll
- **Makeup:** Peter Frampton, Paul Pattison, and Lois Burwell
- **Sound Effects Editing:** Lon Bender and Per Hallberg

Mel Gibson (William Wallace) leads the charge of stalwart Scotsmen against the army of King Edward I of England.

LEAVING LAS VEGAS
Initial Productions, M-G-M / United Artists

- **Best Actor:** Nicholas Cage

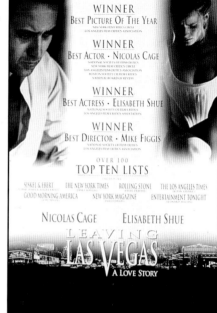

Best Actor Nicolas Cage and love interest Elisabeth Shue.

DEAD MAN WALKING
Working Title / Havoc, Gramercy

- **Best Actress:** Susan Sarandon

Susan Sarandon strives to save the soul of condemned criminal Sean Penn.

THE USUAL SUSPECTS
Blue Parrot, Gramercy

- **Best Supporting Actor:** Kevin Spacey
- **Writing (Screenplay written directly for the screen):** Christopher McQuarrie

Kevin Pollak, Stephen Baldwin, Benicio Del Toro, Gabriel Byrne and Kevin Spacey in a police line-up.

SENSE AND SENSIBILITY
Mirage, Columbia

- **Writing (Screenplay based on material previously produced or published):** Emma Thompson

Emma Thompson and Kate Winslet are two 19th century English sisters whose approach to the opposite sex is quite different.

MIGHTY APHRODITE
Sweetheart, Miramar

- **Best Actress:** Mira Sorvino

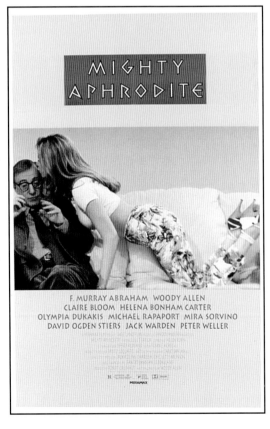

Mira Sorvino plays the mother of a child given up for adoption, who is sought out by the adoptive father, played by Woody Allen.

RESTORATION
Segue / Avenue Pictures / Oxford Film Company, Miramax

- **Art Direction–Set Decoration:** Eugenio Zanetti
- **Costume Design:** James Acheson

Top to bottom: Robert Downey Jr., Polly Walker, Meg Ryan, and Sam Neill star in this 1660s English historical drama.

APOLLO 13

Imagine, Universal

- **Film Editing:** Mike Hill and Dan Hanley
- **Sound:** Rick Dior, Steve Pederson, Scott Millan, and David MacMillan

Bill Paxton, Kevin Bacon, and Tom Hanks trouble shoot aboard Apollo 13.

POCAHONTAS

Disney, Buena Vista

- **Music (Song):** "Colors of the Wind." Music by Alan Menken. Lyric by Stephen Schwartz.
- **Music (Original Musical or Comedy Score):** Music by Alan Menken; lyrics by Stephen Schwartz; orchestral score by Alan Menken.

Pocahantas shows John Smith the way.

THE POSTMAN (IL POSTINO)

Cecchi Gori Group Tiger Cinematografica Production / Pentafilm / Esterno Mediterraneo / Blue Dahlia, Miramax

- **Music (Original Dramatic Score):** Luis Enrique Bacalov

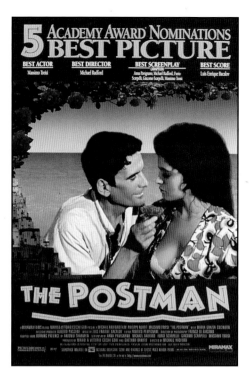

Massimo Troisi (the postman) is scared, yet interested in local girl Maria Grazia Cucinotta.

BABE

Kennedy Miller Pictures, Universal

- **Visual Effects:** Scott E. Anderson, Charles Gibson, Neal Scanlon and John Cox

An eccentric farmer, James Cromwell, forms a bond with this smiling piglet.

ANNE FRANK REMEMBERED
Jon Blair Film Company Ltd., Production; Sony Pictures Classics

- **Documentary (Feature):** Jon Blair, producer

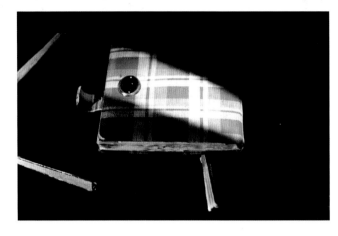

Anne Frank's diary survived the war, and told the story upon which this film was based.

ONE SURVIVOR REMEMBERS
Home Box Office and the United States Holocaust Memorial Museum Production

- **Documentary (Short Subject):** Kary Antholis, producer

ANTONIA'S LINE
The Netherlands

- **Foreign Language Film**

Veerle Van Overloop (Antonia) raises her daughter in Holland after World War II.

A CLOSE SHAVE
Aardman Animations Ltd. Production

- **Short Film (Animated):** Nick Park

Wallace and Gromit are about to have a close shave.

LIEBERMAN IN LOVE
Chanticleer Films

- **Short Film (Live Action):** Christine Lahti and Jana Sue Memel, producers

TOY STORY
Disney / Pixar, Buena Vista

- **Special Achievement Award:** For leadership resulting in the first feature-length computer-animated film: John Lasseter

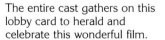

The entire cast gathers on this lobby card to herald and celebrate this wonderful film.

1996

THE ENGLISH PATIENT
Tiger Moth, Miramax

- **Best Picture:** Produced by Saul Zaentz
- **Best Supporting Actress:** Juliette Binoche
- **Direction:** Anthony Minghella
- **Art Direction–Set Decoration:** Stuart Craig and Stephanie McMillan
- **Cinematography:** John Seale
- **Costume Design:** Ann Roth
- **Film Editing:** Walter Murch
- **Music (Original Dramatic Score):** Gabriel Yared
- **Sound:** Walter Murch, Mark Berger, David Parker, and Chris Newman

SHINE
Momentum Films, Fine Line Features

- **Best Actor:** Geoffrey Rush

Geoffrey Rush plays David Helfgott, the brilliant musician who suffered a debilitating nervous breakdown at the peak of his career. Noah Taylor plays Helfgott as a younger man. Lynne Redgrave is in the cast as well.

Award winner Juliette Binoche takes care of the English patient.

FARGO
Working Title, Gramercy

- **Best Actress:** Frances McDormand
- **Writing (Screenplay written directly for the screen):** Ethan Coen, Joel Coen

A "film noir" set in North Dakota and Minnesota, involving a murder mystery with many surprise events.

283

JERRY MAGUIRE
Tri-Star

- **Best Supporting Actor:** Cuba Gooding, Jr.

Cuba Gooding Jr. plays an Arizona Cardinals wide receiver who, along with his sports agent played by Tom Cruise, is extremely concerned about his future and his money.

THE NUTTY PROFESSOR
Imagine, Universal

- **Makeup:** Rick Baker and David Leroy Anderson

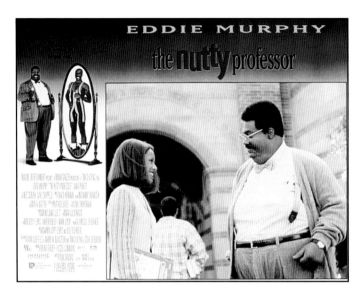

This amusing film features Eddie Murphy as obese Professor Sherman Klump, who is able to lose a large amount of weight to woo graduate student Jada Pinkett.

SLING BLADE
Shooting Gallery, Miramax

- **Writing (Screenplay based on material previously produced or published):** Billy Bob Thornton

Billy Bob Thornton plays a tragic and simple soul who, after being in an asylum for twenty-five years, goes home and faces some unhappy turns of events.

EVITA
Hollywood Pictures / Cinergi Pictures, Buena Vista

- **Music (Song):** "You Must Love Me." Music by Andrew Lloyd Webber. Lyrics by Tim Rice.

Madonna (as Evita Peron) and Antonio Banderas sing a duet.

EMMA
Matchmaker Films / Haft Entertainment, Miramax

- **Music (Original Musical or Comedy Score):** Rachel Portman

Gwyneth Paltrow plays a matchmaker who pays attention to everyone else's love life, neglecting her own.

INDEPENDENCE DAY
20th Century-Fox

- **Visual Effects:** Volker Engel, Douglas Smith, Clay Pinney, and Joseph Viskocil

Will Smith and Jeff Goldblum join forces to defeat an invasion from another planet.

THE GHOST AND THE DARKNESS
Douglas / Reuther, Paramount

- **Sound Effects Editing:** Bruce Stambler

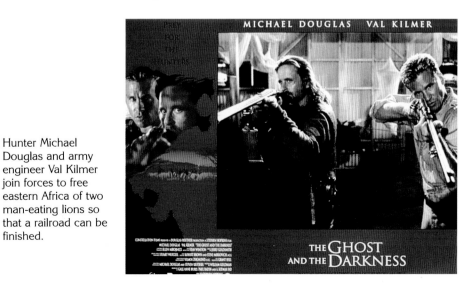

Hunter Michael Douglas and army engineer Val Kilmer join forces to free eastern Africa of two man-eating lions so that a railroad can be finished.

WHEN WE WERE KINGS
DASfilms Ltd. Production; Grammercy

- **Documentary (Feature):** Leon Gast and David Sonenberg, producers

Muhammad Ali poses for fans outside a bus in Zaire in 1974.

BREATHING LESSONS: THE LIFE AND WORK OF MARK O'BRIEN
Inscrutable Films / Pacific News Service Production

- **Documentary (Short Subject):** Jessica Yu

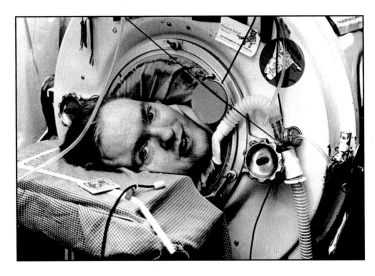

The picture of Mark O'Brien tells the story.

KOLYA
Czech Republic

- **Foreign Language Film**

Zdenek Sverak and Andrej Chalimon are the stars.

QUEST
Thomas Stellmach Animation Production

- **Short Film (Animated):** Tyron Montgomery and Thomas Stellmach, producers

DEAR DIARY
Dream Works SKG Production

- **Short Film (Live Action):** David Frankel and Barry Jossen, producers.

Renato Carpentieri, Claudia Della Seta, Lorenzo Alessandri, and Nanni Moretti star in this Italian film.

AS GOOD AS IT GETS
Gracie Films, Tri-Star

- **Best Actor:** Jack Nicholson
- **Best Actress:** Helen Hunt

TITANIC
Lightstorm Entertainment, 20ᵗʰ Century-Fox and Paramount

- **Best Picture:** Produced by James Cameron and Jon Landau
- **Direction:** James Cameron
- **Cinematography:** Russell Carpenter
- **Art Direction–Set Decoration:** Peter Lamont and Michael Ford
- **Costume Design:** Deborah L. Scott
- **Sound:** Gary Rydstrom, Tom Johnson, Gary Summers, and Mark Ulano
- **Film Editing:** Conrad Buff, James Cameron, and Richard A. Harris
- **Sound Effects Editing:** Tom Bellfort and Christopher Boyes
- **Music (Song):** "My Heart Will Go On." Music by James Horner. Lyrics by Will Jennings.
- **Music (Original Dramatic Score):** James Horner
- **Visual Effects:** Robert Legato, Mark Lasoff, Thomas L. Fisher, and Michael Kanfer.

Helen Hunt and Jack Nicholson spar and flirt throughout this love story about two people dealing with serious obstacles to a stable relationship, such as the main character's obsessive-compulsive disorder.

AS GOOD AS IT GETS

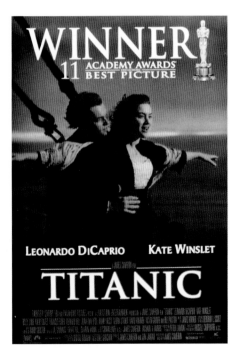

Lovers Kate Winslet and Leonardo DiCaprio are on top of the world before disaster strikes the Titanic.

GOOD WILL HUNTING
Be Gentlemen, Miramax

- **Best Supporting Actor:** Robin Williams
- **Writing (Screenplay written directly for the screen):** Ben Affleck and Matt Damon

Matt Damon and Robin Williams become better friends.

L.A. CONFIDENTIAL
Arnon-Milchan / David L. Wolper, Warner Brothers

- **Best Supporting Actress:** Kim Basinger
- **Writing (Screenplay based on material from another medium):** Brian Helgeland and Curtis Hanson

Kim Basinger plays a prostitute who seduces detective Russell Crowe in this 1950s-style "film noir." (Spanish lobby card)

THE FULL MONTY
Redwave Films, Fox Searchlight

- **Music (Original Musical or Comedy Score):** Anne Dudley

Robert Carlye, Tom Wilkinson, Hugo Speer, Steve Huison, and Paul Barber dance before showing the full monty.

MEN IN BLACK
Amblin Entertainment, Columbia

- **Makeup:** Rick Baker and David Leroy Anderson

Will Smith and Tommy Lee Jones join forces to combat aliens who inhabit the bodies of humans.

GERI'S GAME
Pixar Animation Studios Production

- **Short Film (Animated):** Produced by Jan Pinkava

VISAS AND VIRTUE
Cedar Grove Production

- **Short Film (Live Action):** Produced by Chris Tashima and Chris Donahue

A STORY OF HEALING
Dewey-Obenchain Films Production

- **Documentary (Short Subject):** Produced by Donna Dewey and Carol Pasternak

THE LONG WAY HOME
Moriah Films Production at the Simon Wiesenthal Center, Seventh Art

- **Documentary (Feature):** Produced by Rabbi Marvin Hier and Richard Trank

CHARACTER
First Floor Features Production, Sony Pictures Classic

- **Foreign Language Film** (The Netherlands)

Fedja van Huet and Tamar van den Dop are in character.

1998

SHAKESPEARE IN LOVE
Miramax Films, Universal, Bedford Falls Co. Production

- **Best Picture:** Produced by David Parfitt, Donna Gigliotti, Harvey Weinstein, Edward Zwick and Marc Norman
- **Best Actress:** Gwyneth Paltrow
- **Best Supporting Actress:** Judi Dench
- **Writing (Screenplay written directly for the screen):** Marc Norman and Tom Stoppard
- **Art Direction:** Martin Childs; Set Decoration: Jill Quertier
- **Costume Design:** Sandy Powell
- **Music (Original Musical or Comedy Score):** Stephen Warbeck

LIFE IS BEAUTIFUL
Melampo Cinematografica Production, Miramax Films

- **Best Actor:** Roberto Benigni
- **Music (Original Dramatic Score):** Nicola Piovani
- **Foreign Language Film:** Italy

Roberto Benigni and Nicoletta Braschi share a tender moment while life was still beautiful in Italy pre-World War II .

Queen Judi Dench in Shakespearean splendor. Gwyneth Paltrow is at lower right.

AFFLICTION
Tormenta Production, Lions Gate Films

- **Best Supporting Actor:** James Coburn

James Coburn and Nick Nolte, as father and son, are involved with a New Hampshire murder mystery.

289

SAVING PRIVATE RYAN

Amblin Entertainment Production in association with Mutual Film Company, Dream Works Pictures and Paramount Pictures

- **Direction:** Steven Spielberg
- **Film Editing:** Michael Kahn
- **Sound:** Gary Rydstrom, Gary Summers, Andy Nelson and Ronald Judkins
- **Sound Effects Editing:** Gary Rydstrom and Richard Hymns
- **Cinematography:** Janusz Kaminski

Tom Hanks, Matt Damon (as Private Ryan), and Ed Burns defend a small town against the Germans on their way to getting Private Ryan home from the war safely.

GODS AND MONSTERS

Regent Pictures, Lions Gate Films

- **Writing (Screenplay based on material previously produced or published):** Bill Condon

Ian McKellan and Rosalind Ayres on the set.

ELIZABETH

Working Title Production, Gramercy Pictures

- **Makeup:** Jenny Shircore

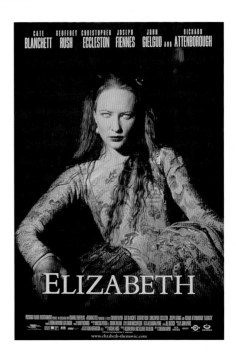

Cate Blanchett , as Elizabeth, emerged from her masculine clothing into regal royal splendor.

THE PRINCE OF EGYPT
Dreamworks SKG Production

- **Music (Original Song):** "When You Believe." Music and lyric by Stephen Schwartz

An animated film with a splendid song.

WHAT DREAMS MAY COME
Interscope Communications Production in association with Metafilmics, Polygram

- **Visual Effects:** Joel Hynek, Nicholas Brooks, Stuart Robertson and Kevin Mack

Robin Williams with some of the film's spectacular visual effects in the background.

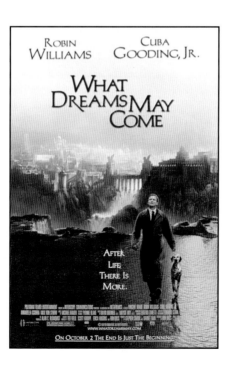

THE LAST DAYS
Survivors of the Shoah Visual History Foundation Production. October Films.

- **Documentary (Feature):** James Moll and Ken Lipper, producers

Five Hungarian survivors recount their horrible stories of massacre, torture, slavery, and death in World War II.

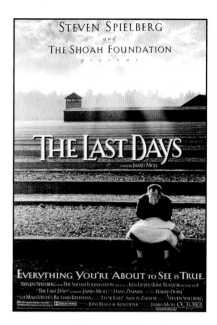

THE PERSONALS: IMPROVISATIONS ON ROMANCE IN THE GOLDEN YEARS
Keiko Ibi Film Production

- **Documentary (Short Subject):** Keiko Ibi

This happy couple dances in their golden years.

BUNNY
Blue Sky Studios, Inc. Production
- **Short Film (Animated):** Chris Wedge

ELECTION NIGHT (VALGAFTEN)
M&M Production

- **Short Film (Live Action):** Kim Magnusson and Anders Thomas Jensen

1999

AMERICAN BEAUTY

Jinks / Cohen Company Production, Dream Works

- **Best Picture:** Bruce Cohen and Dan Jinks, producers
- **Best Actor:** Kevin Spacey
- **Direction:** Sam Mendes
- **Writing (Screenplay written directly for the screen):** Alan Ball
- **Cinematography:** Conrad L. Hall

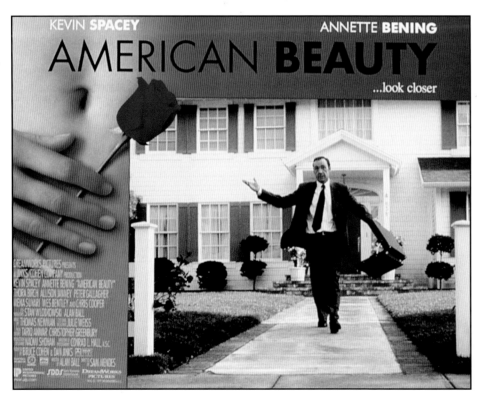

Kevin Spacey doesn't give a darn as both his briefcase and his family life are coming apart!

BOYS DON'T CRY

Killer Films/Hart-Sharp Entertainment Production. Fox Searchlight.

- **Best Actress:** Hilary Swank

A somewhat tragic film about white youth gang crime in Nebraska.

THE CIDER HOUSE RULES

Film Colony Production, Miramax Films

- **Best Supporting Actor:** Michael Caine
- **Writing (Screenplay based on material previously produced or published):** John Irving

Tobey Maguire and Charlize Theron become lovers while her husband is in the service during World War II.

GIRL, INTERRUPTED

Red Wagon / Columbia Pictures Production

- **Best Supporting Actress:** Angelina Jolie

Angelina Jolie is an inmate of a mental institution in this film.

SLEEPY HOLLOW
Scott Rudin / American Zoetrope Production, Paramount and Mandalay

- **Art Direction:** Rick Heinrichs; Set Direction: Peter Young

Johnny Depp and Christina Ricci prepare to fight the headless horseman.

THE MATRIX
Matrix Films Pty Ltd. Production, Warner Brothers

- **Film Editing:** Zach Staenberg
- **Sound:** John Reitz, Gregg Rudloff, David Campbell and David Lee
- **Sound Effects Editing:** Dane A. Davis
- **Visual Effects:** John Gaeta, Janek Sirrs, Steve Courtley and Jon Thum

Carrie Ann Moss and Keanu Reeves join forces against renegade government agents.

TOPSY-TURVY
Simon Channing – Williams Production, USA Films

- **Costume Design:** Lindy Hemming
- **Makeup:** Christine Blundell and Trefor Proud

Allan Corduner and Jim Broadbent take their bows.

TARZAN
Walt Disney Pictures Production , Buena Vista

- **Music (Original Song):** "You'll Be In My Heart." Music and lyrics by Phil Collins

Flawless animation combines with outstanding music in this timeless tale.

THE RED VIOLIN
Rhombus Media Production, Lions Gate Films

- **Music (Original Score):** John Corigliano

Samuel L. Jackson is in a difficult situation as he protects the red violin.

ONE DAY IN SEPTEMBER
Arthur Cohn Production

- **Documentary (Feature):** Arthur Cohn and Kevin MacDonald, producers

Tending the grave of a loved one.

KING GIMP
Whiteford-Hadary / University of Maryland / Tapestry International Production

- **Documentary (Short Subject):** Susan Hannah Hadary and William A. Whiteford, producers

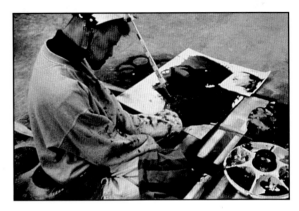

Dan Keplinger paints to his fullest potential despite his disability.

ALL ABOUT MY MOTHER
El Deseo S.A. / Renn / France 2 Cinema Production, Sony Pictures Classics (Spain)

- **Foreign Language Film**

Cecelia Roth in a starring role.

THE OLD MAN AND THE SEA
Productions Pascal Blais / Imagica Corp. / Dentsu Tech / NHK Enterprise 21 / Panorama Studio of Yaroslavl Production

- **Short Film (Animated):** Alexander Petrov, producer

MY MOTHER DREAMS THE SATAN'S DISCIPLES IN NEW YORK
Kickstart Production, American Film Institute

- **Short Film (Live Action):** Barbara Schock and Tammy Tiehel, producers

2000

GLADIATOR

Douglas Wick in association with Scott Free Production, Dream Works and Universal

- **Best Picture:** Douglas Wick, David Franzoni and Branko Lustig, producers
- **Best Actor:** Russell Crowe
- **Costume Design:** Janty Yates
- **Sound:** Scott Millan, Bob Beemer and Ken Weston
- **Visual Effects:** John Nelson, Neil Corbould, Tim Burke and Rob Harvey

ERIN BROCKOVICH

Jersey Films Production, Universal and Columbia

- **Best Actress:** Julia Roberts

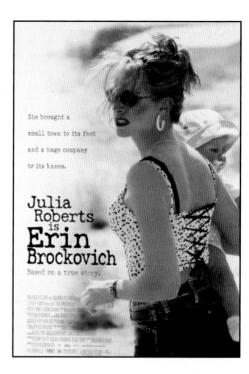

Julia Roberts takes on big business and wins.

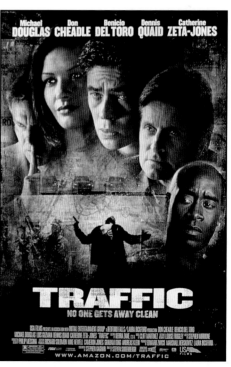

TRAFFIC

Bedford Falls / Lauara Bickford Production, USA Films

- **Best Supporting Actor:** Benicio Del Toro
- **Direction:** Steven Soderbergh
- **Writing (Screenplay based on material previously produced or published):** Stephan Gaghan
- **Film Editing:** Stephen Mirrione

Left to right: Dennis Quaid, Catherine Zeta-Jones, Benicio Del Toro, Michael Douglas, and Don Cheadle star in this film about drug trafficking.

Russell Crowe triumphs over soldiers and tigers in the Roman gladitorial arena.

POLLOCK

Brant / Allen Films / Zeke Films / Fred Berner Films Production, Sony Pictures Classics

- **Best Supporting Actress:** Marcia Gay Harden

Marcia Gay Harden shares an intimate restaurant conversation with Ed Harris.

ALMOST FAMOUS

Vinyl Films Production, Dream Works and Columbia

- **Writing (Screenplay written directly for the screen):** Cameron Crowe

Kate Hudson becomes almost famous.

CROUCHING TIGER, HIDDEN DRAGON

Zoom Hunt International Productions, Sony Pictures Classics

- **Art Direction:** Tim Yip
- **Cinematography:** Peter Pau
- **Music (Original Score):** Tan Dun
- **Foreign Language Film** (Taiwan)

This is a scene from near the conclusion of this exciting adventure film. Chow Yun Fat holds his dying love, Zhang Ziyi.

U-571

Dino De Laurentis Production, Universal and Studio Canal

- **Sound Editing:** Jon Johnson

Matthew McConaughey, Erik Palladino and Jack Noseworthy search for the enemy.

DR. SEUSS' HOW THE GRINCH STOLE CHRISTMAS

Universal Pictures and Imagine Entertainment Production, Universal

- **Makeup:** Rick Baker and Gail Ryan

This is an advance one-sheet poster featuring Jim Carey as the Grinch, whose goal is to steal Christmas from the little Whos down in their town of Whoville.

WONDER BOYS

Scott Rudin / Curtis Hanson Production, Paramount and Mutual Film Company

- **Music (Original Song):** "Things Have Changed." Music and lyrics by Bob Dylan

Michael Douglas, an aging writer, struggles within himself about his abilities and his work.

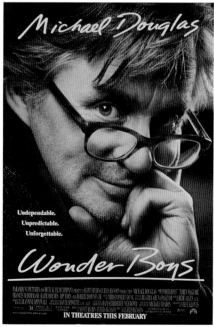

FATHER AND DAUGHTER

Ciné Té Filmproductie by/ Cloudrunner Ltd. Production

- **Short Film (Animated):** Michael Dudok de Wit, producer

QUIERO SER (I WANT TO BE...)

Mondragon Films Production

- **Short Film (Live Action):** Florian Gallenberger, producer

INTO THE ARMS OF STRANGERS: STORIES OF THE KINDERTRANSPORT

Sabine Films Production, Warner Brothers

- Documentary (Feature): **Mark Jonathan Harris and Deborah Oppenheimer, producers**

BIG MAMA

Birthmark Production

- **Documentary (Short Subject):** Tracy Seretean, producer

2001

A Beautiful Mind
Universal Pctures and Imagine Entertainment Production, Universal and Dream Works

- **Best Picture:** Brian Grazer and Ron Howard, Producers
- **Best Supporting Actress:** Jennifer Connelly
- **Direction:** Ron Howard
- **Writing (Screenplay based on material previously produced or published):** Akiva Goldsman

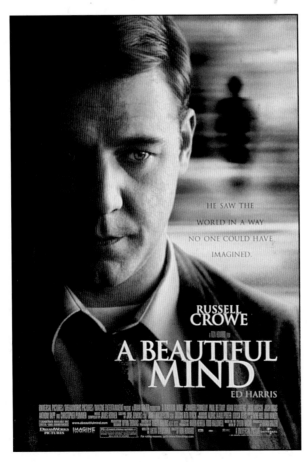

Russell Crowe as the brilliant scientist John Nash, whose battle with schizophrenia is chronicled in this Academy Award® winning film.

Iris
Mirage Enterprises, Robert Fox / Scott Rudin Production, Miramax Films

- **Best Supporting Actor:** Jim Broadbent

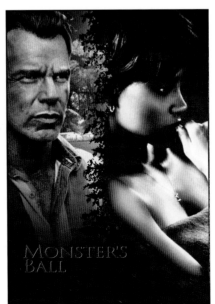

Training Day
Training Day Production, Warner Brothers

- **Best Actor:** Denzel Washington

Ethan Hawke, as a rookie cop, and Denzel Washington, an undercover narcotics agent, battle the bad guys with an interesting twist.

Award nominees Judi Dench and Kate Winslet both portray Iris Murdoch in this biographical study of the writer's life. Jim Broadbent stars brilliantly as Murdoch's love of 40 years, John Bayley, who wrote the two books from which this film was made. (Press ad)

Monster's Ball
Monster Productions, Lion's Gate Films

- **Best Actress:** Halle Berry

Halle Berry and Billy Bob Thornton help each other during hard times.

GOSFORD PARK

Sandcastle 5 in association with Chicagofilms and Medusa Film Production, USA Films

- **Writing (Screenplay written directly for the screen):** Julian Fellowes

Fabulous cast for a British murder mystery in the old style.

SHREK

PDI / DreamWorks Production, DreamWorks

- **Animated Feature Film:** Aron Warner, producer

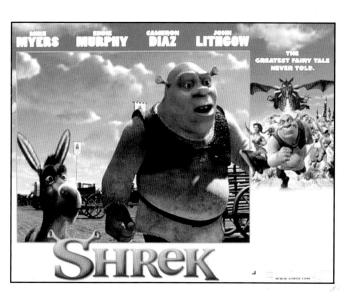

Shrek and his long-eared friend help to bring "the greatest fairy tale ever told" to life!

THE LORD OF THE RINGS: THE FELLOWSHIP OF THE RING

New Line Cinema and Wingnut Films Production, New Line

- **Cinematography:** Andrew Lesnie
- **Makeup:** Peter Owen and Richard Taylor
- **Visual Effects:** Jim Rygiel, Randall William Cook, Richard Taylor and Mark Stetson
- **Music (Original Score):** Howard Shore

Left to right: Liv Tyler, Elijah Wood, and Ian McKellan fight the forces of evil.

MOULIN ROUGE

20th Century-Fox Production, 20th Century-Fox

- **Costume Design:** Catherine Martin and Angus Strathie, producers
- **Art Direction:** Catherine Martin; Set Direction: Brigitte Broch

Nicole Kidman and Ewan McGregor serenade Paris.

BLACK HAWK DOWN
Revolution Studios Production, Sony Pictures Releasing

- **Film Editing:** Pietro Scalia
- **Sound:** Michael Minkler, Myron Nettinga and Chris Munro

Josh Hartnett tries to figure out how to save his fellow Marines in Somalia.

MONSTERS, INC.
Walt Disney Pictures / Pixar Animation Studios Production, Buena Vista

- **Music (Original Song):** "If I Didn't Have You." Music and lyrics by Randy Newman.

Sulley and Mike Wazowski are amazed.

NO MAN'S LAND
Noé Productions / Fabrica Cinema / Man's Films / Counihan Villiers Production / Studio Maj / Casablanca Productions. United Artists through M-G-M (Bosnia and Herzegovina)

- **Foreign Language Film** (Bosnia and Herzegovina)

Branko Djuric and Rene Bitorajac wave white shirts for peace.

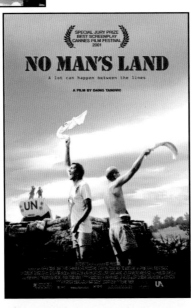

PEARL HARBOR
Touchstone Pictures / Jerry Bruckheimer Films Production, Buena Vista

- **Sound Editing:** George Watters II, and Christopher Boyes

The December 7, 1941 attack on Pearl Harbor brought the United States into World War II.

MURDER ON A SUNDAY MORNING
Maha Productions / Path, Doc/ France 2/ HBO Productions

- **Documentary (Feature):** Jean-Xavier de Lestrade and Denis Poncet, producers

THOTH
Amateur Rabbit Production

- **Documentary (Short Subject):** Sarah Kernochan and Lynn Appelle, producers

FOR THE BIRDS
Pixar Animation Studios Production

- **Short Film (Animated):** Ralph Eggleston, producer

THE ACCOUNTANT
Ginny Mule Pictures Production

- **Short Film (Live Action):** Ray McKinnon and Lisa Blount, producers

BIBLIOGRAPHY

Academy of Motion Picture Arts and Sciences Center For Motion Picture Study, 333 South La Cienega Boulevard, Beverly Hills, California, 90211

Academy of Motion Picture Arts and Sciences Margaret Herrick Library, 333 South La Cienega Boulevard, Beverly Hills, California, 90211

Halliwell, Leslie. *Halliwell's Film Guide 1996,* Great Britain: HarperCollins*Publishers,* 1995.

Halliwell, Leslie. *The Filmgoer's Companion,* New York, New York: Avon Books, 1978.

Hershenson, Bruce. *Academy Award ® Winners' Movie Posters,* West Plains, Missouri: Published by Bruce Hershenson.

Hershenson, Bruce. *Best Pictures' Movie Posters,* West Plains, Missouri: Published by Bruce Hershenson, 1999.

Kisch, John. *2001 Movie Poster Price Alamanac,* Poughkeepsie, New York: Netpub, 2001.

Kobal, John and Wilson, V.A. *For Your Pleasure: The Golden Age of Cinema Lobby Cards,* London, England: Atrium Press, 1982.

Maltin, Leonard. *1997 Movie & Video Guide,* New York, New York: Penguin Books, 1997.

Martin, Mick, and Porter, Marsha. *2001 Video and Movie Guide,* New York, New York: Ballantine Books, 2000.

Osborne, Robert. *Academy Awards ® 1972 Oscar ® Annual,* LaHabra, California: ESE California, 1972.

Osborne, Robert. *Academy Awards ® 1973 Oscar ® Annual,* LaHabra, California: ESE California, 1973.

Osborne, Robert. *Academy Awards ® 1974 Oscar ® Annual,* LaHabra, California: ESE California, 1974.

Osborne, Robert. *Academy Awards ® 1975 Oscar ® Annual,* LaHabra, California: ESE California, 1975.

Osborne, Robert. *70 Years of the Oscar ®,* New York, New York: Abbeville Press, 1999.

Scott, Kathryn Lee. *Lobby Cards, The Classic Comedies,* Los Angeles, California: Pomegranate Press, Ltd., 1988.

Scott, Kathryn Lee. *Lobby Cards, The Classic Films,* Los Angeles, California: Pomegranate Press, Ltd., 1987.

PRICE GUIDE

Abyss, The (one-sheet), $50-75
Accidental Tourist, The (one-sheet), $60-80
Accused, The, $30-40
Adventures of Don Juan, $100-150
Adventures of Priscilla, Queen of the Desert, The (One-sheet), $50-75
Adventures of Robin Hood, The, $800-1000
Affliction (One-sheet), $50-75
African Queen, The, $250-300
Age of Innocence, The, $30-40
Air Force, $75-100
Airport, $60-75
Aladdin, $40-50
Alamo, The, $150-200
Alaskan Eskimo, The, $50-75
Alexander's Ragtime Band, $150-200
Alice Doesn't Live Here Anymore, $40-60
Alien, $100-125
Aliens, $75-100
All About Eve, $250-300
All About My Mother (Color 8 x 10" still), $25-30
All Quiet on the Western Front, $400-500
All That Jazz, $25-50
All That Money Can Buy, $250-300
All the King's Men (Crawford / Derek), $100-125
All the King's Men (McCambridge / Ireland), $40-50
All the President's Men, $75-100
Almost Famous (Color 8 x 10" still), $20-25
Ama Girls (8 x 10" still), $20-25
Amadeus, $40-50
Amarcord, $75-100
America America, $40-50
American Beauty, $40-50
American in Paris, An, $300-400
American Werewolf in London, An, $40-50
Anastasia, $100-125
Anchors Aweigh, $150-200
Anna and the King of Siam, $100-150
Anne Frank Remembered (8 x 10" still), $15-20
Anne of the Thousand Days, $60-75
Annie Get Your Gun, $100-125
Annie Hall, $75-100
Anthony Adverse, $100-150
Antonia's Line (Color 8 x 10" still), $20-25
Apartment, The , $50-75
Apocalypse Now, $75-100
Apollo 13, $30-40
Arise My Love, $100-150

Around the World In Eighty Days, $100-125
Arthur, $75-100
Artie Shaw: Time is All You've Got (8 x 10" still), $20-25
As Good as it Gets, $40-50
Assault, The (8 x 10" still), $20-25
Awful Truth, The, $250-300
Babe, $30-40
Babette's Feast (8 x 10" still), $20-25
Bachelor and the Bobby Soxer, The, $200-250
Back to the Future, $60-80
Bad and the Beautiful, The, $75-100
Bad Girl, $150-200
Barefoot Contessa, The, $100-150
Barry Lyndon, $50-75
Batman, $40-50
Battle of Midway (8 x 10" still), $15
Battleground, $60-75
Bear Country, $60-75
Beautiful Mind, A (One-sheet), $30-40
Beauty and the Beast, $75-90
Becket, $75-100
Bedknobs and Broomsticks, $60-80
Beetlejuice, $40-50
Being There, $40-50
Belle Epoque (8 x 10 color still), $25-30
Bells of St. Mary's, The, $150-200
Ben Hur, $75-100
Best Boy (one-sheet), $75-100
Best Years of Our Lives, The, $150-200
Bicycle Thief, The, $75-100
Big Broadcast of 1938, $400-500
Big Country, The, $125-150
Big House, The, $200-250
Bill and Coo, $100-125
Bird (One-sheet), $60-80
Bishop's Wife, The, $150-200
Black and White in Color, $60-75
Black Fox (8 x 10" still), $30
Black Hawk Down (One-sheet), $30-40
Black Narcissus, $200-250
Black Orpheus, $100-125
Black Stallion, The, $40-50
Black Swan, The, $150-200
Blithe Spirit, $150-200
Blood and Sand, $250-300
Blood on the Sun, $200-250
Blossoms in the Dust, $150-200
Blue Sky, $30-40
Body and Soul, $200-250
Bonnie and Clyde, $50-75
Born Free, $40-50
Born on the Fourth of July, $40-50
Born Yesterday, $50-75
Bound for Glory, $40-50
Boy and His Dog, The (8 x 10" still), $15
Boys Don't Cry (One-sheet), $50-75
Boys Town, $200-250
Bram Stoker's Dracula (One-sheet), $75-100
Brave One, $30-40
Braveheart, $40-60

Breakfast at Tiffany's, $200-250
Breaking Away, $60-75
Breaking the Sound Barrier, $75-100
Breathing Lessons (Color 8 x 10" still), $15-20
Bridge of San Luis Rey, The, $150-200
Bridge on the River Kwai, The, $75-100
Bridges at Toko-Ri, The, $75-100
Broadway Melody of 1936, $250-300
Broadway Melody,The, $1500-2000
Broken Lance, $75-100
Buddy Holly Story, The, $60-75
Bugsy, $40-50
Bullets Over Broadway (One-sheet), $80-100
Bullitt, $100-125
Burnt by the Sun (Color 8 x 10" still), $20-25
Butch Cassidy and the Sundance Kid, $100-150
Butterfield 8, $75-100
Butterflies are Free, $75-100
Cabaret, $100-125
Cactus Flower, $50-75
Calamity Jane, $75-100
California Suite, $40-60
Call Me Madam, $100-150
Camelot, $75-100
Candidate, The, $75-100
Captain Carey, $100-125
Captains Courageous, $300-400
Casablanca, $4000-5000
Cat Ballou, $100-150
Cavalcade, $400-500
Champ, The, $200-250
Champion, $150-200
Character (Color 8 x 10" still), $20-25
Charge of the Light Brigade, The, $1200-1500
Chariots of Fire, $50-75
Charly, $50-75
Children of a Lesser God, $30-40
Chinatown (internation release lobby card), $75-100
Cider House Rules, The (One-sheet), $75-100
Cimarron, $250-300
Cinema Paradiso (8 x 10" still), $20-25
Circus, The, $600-800
Citizen Kane, $1200-1500
City Slickers (Video posterl), $20-25
Cleopatra, $400-500
Climbing the Matterhorn (One-sheet), $250-300
Close Encounters of the Third Kind, $50-75
Close Shave, A (Color 8 x 10" still), $20-25
Closely Watched Trains, $75-100
Coal Miner's Daughter, $50-75
Cocoon, $30-40
Color of Money, The (One-sheet), $200-250
Come and Get It, $200-250
Come Back Little Sheba, $150-200
Coming Home, $60-80
Cool Hand Luke, $100-125

Coquette, $250-300
Country Cousin (8 x 10" still), $30
Country Girl, The, $100-150
Cover Girl, $200-250
Cowboy and the Lady, The, $300-400
Crash Dive, $300-400
Cries and Whispers (One-sheet), $150-200
Critic, The (Half-sheet), $200-250
Cromwell, $75-100
Crouching Tiger, Hidden Dragon, $40-50
Crying Game, The (Color 8 x 10" still), $20-25
Cyrano de Bergerac, $250-300
Cyrano de Bergerac (8x10" still), $20-25
Damsel In Distress, The, $800-1000
Dances With Wolves, $30-40
Dangerous, $1500-2000
Dangerous Liaisons, $75-100
Dangerous Moves (One-sheet), $100-150
Dark Angel, The, $300-400
Darling, $75-100
Dawn Patrol, The, $300-350
Day For Night, $75-100
Days of Heaven, $40-60
Days of Wine and Roses, $75-100
Dead Man Walking (One-sheet), $75-100
Dead Poet's Society , $40-50
Dear Diary (Color 8 x 10" still), $20-25
Death Becomes Her, $40-50
Death on the Nile, $100-150
Deer Hunter, The, $75-100
Defiant Ones, The, $50-75
Der Fuehrer's Face (One-sheet), $2500-3000
Dersu Uzala (One-sheet), $150-200
Desert Victory, $200-250
Design for Death, $100-150
Designing Woman, $50-75
Destination Moon, $250-300
Diary of Anne Frank, The, $100-150
Dick Tracy, (8 x 10" color still), $15-25
Dirty Dancing, $30-40
Dirty Dozen, The, $100-150
Discreet Charm of the Bourgeoisie, The (One-sheet), $75-100
Disraeli, $250-300
Divine Lady,The, $200-250
Divorce - Italian Syle, $50-75
Divorcee, The, $250-300
Doctor Doolittle, $50-75
Doctor Zhivago, $100-125
Dodsworth, $300-400
Dog Day Afternoon, $50-75
Double Life, A, $150-200
Dove, The, $100-150
Dr. Jekyll and Mister Hyde, $7000-8000
Dr. Seuss' How the Grinch Stole Christmas (Advance One-sheet), $40-50
Driving Miss Daisy (One-sheet), $40-50
Dumbo, $800-1000
E.T. The Extra-Terrestrial, $40-50
Earthquake, $50-75

East of Eden, $300-350
Easter Parade, $200-250
Ed Wood, $50-75
Educating Peter (8 x 10" still), $15-20
Eleanor Roosevelt Story (One-sheet), $75-100
Elizabeth (One-sheet), $50-75
Elmer Gantry, $75-100
Emma (One-sheet), $75-100
Empire Strikes Back, The, $75-100
Enemy Below, The, $50-75
English Patient, The (Color 8 x 10" still), $20-25
Erin Brockovich (One-sheet), $50-75
Eskimo, $300-400
Evita, $30-40
Exodus, $75-100
Exorcist, The, $75-100
Facts of Life, The, $75-100
Fame, $40-60
Fanny and Alexander (One-sheet), $40-50
Fantasia, $1200-1500
Fantastic Voyage, $75-100
Farewell to Arms, A, $300-400
Fargo (One-sheet), $50-75
Farmer's Daughter, The, $100-150
Father Goose, $75-100
Federico Fellini's 8 1/2, $100-150
Fellini's Casanova, $50-75
Ferdinand the Bull, $1500-2000
Fiddler on the Roof, $75-100
Fighting Lady, The , $200-250
Fish Called Wanda, A, $30-40
Fisher King, The, $30-40
Flashdance, $30-40
Flowers and Trees (8 x 10" still), $30
Fly, The, $30-40
Folies Bergère, $300-400
For Whom the Bell Tolls, $150-200
Forbidden Games (8 x 10" still), $30
Forrest Gump, $40-50
Fortune Cookie, The, $75-100
Franz Kafka's It's a Wonderful Life (8 x 10" still), $15-20
Free Soul, A, $400-500
French Connection, The, $75-100
Frenchman's Creek, $150-200
From Here to Eternity, $150-200
Fugitive, The, $30-40
Full Monty, The (Color 8 x 10" still), $20-25
Funny Girl, $100-150
Funny Thing Happened on the Way to the Forum, A, $75-100
Gandhi, $40-50
Garden of Allah, The, $300-400
Garden of the Finzi-Continis, The, $100-125
Gaslight, $150-200
Gate of Hell (One-sheet), $250-300
Gay Divorcee, The, $800-1000
Gentleman's Agreement, $150-200
Gerald McBoing-Boing (8 x 10" still), $25
Get Out Your Handkerchiefs (One-sheet),

$150-200

Ghost (One-sheet), $40-50
Ghost and the Darkness, The, $30-40
Giant, $150-200
Gigi, $75-100
Girl, Interrupted, $30-40
Gladiator, $40-50
Glenn Miller Story, The, $100-125
Glory (8 x 10" still), $25-30
Godfather, Part II, The, $100-150
Godfather, The, $150-200
Gods and Monsters (Color 8 x 10" still), $20-25
Going My Way, $200-250
Gold Diggers of 1935, $300-400
Golden Fish, The (One-sheet), $100-150
Goldfinger, $100-125
Gone With the Wind (Leigh), $1200-1500
Gone With the Wind (McDaniel), $500-600
Good Earth, The, $500-600
Good Fellas (One-sheet), $75-100
Good Will Hunting (Color 8 x 10" still), $20-25
Goodbye Girl, The, $40-60
Goodbye, Mr. Chips, $300-400
Gosford Park (One-sheet), $30-40
Graduate, The, $50-75
Grand Hotel, $1200-1500
Grand Prix, $125-150
Grapes of Wrath, The, $500-600
Great American Cowboy, The, (One-sheet), $100-150
Great Caruso, The, $75-100
Great Expectations, $250-300
Great Gatsby, The, $75-100
Great Lie, The, $250-300
Great McGinty, The, $250-300
Great Race, The, $100-125
Great Waltz, The, $200-250
Great Ziegfeld, The, $700-800
Greatest Show on Earth, The, $150-200
Green Dolphin Street, $100-150
Green Goddess, The (One-sheet), $400-500
Guess Who's Coming to Dinner?, $50-75
Guns of Navarone, The, $75-100
Hamlet, $200-250
Hannah and Her Sisters (One-sheet), $50-75
Harlan County, U.S.A. (8 x 10" still), $15
Harry and The Hendersons, $20-30
Harry and Tonto, $40-60
Harvey, $600-800
Harvey Girls, The , $250-300
Hearts and Minds (8 x 10" still), $15
Heaven Can Wait, $40-60
Heavenly Music (One-sheet), $400-500
Heiress, The, $100-150
Hello Dolly!, $75-100
Hello Frisco Hello, $150-200
Hellstrom Chronicle, The, $40-60
Henry V, $150-200
Henry V (One-sheet), $100-150
Herb Alpert and the Tijuana Brass Double

Feature (One-sheet), $250-300
Here Comes Mr. Jordan, $300-400
Here Comes the Groom, $75-100
High and the Mighty, The, $100-150
High Noon, $250-300
Hindenberg, The, $60-80
Hole in the Head, A, $100-150
Holiday Inn, $300-400
Hospital, The, $75-100
Hotel Terminus (8 x 10" still), $25-30
House I Live In, The (8 x 10" still), $100
House on 92nd Street, The, $150-200
How Green Was My Valley, $300-400
How the West Was Won, $100-150
Howard's End (One-sheet), $75-100
Hud (Neal, Newman), $50-75
Hud (Newman, Douglas, DeWilde), $50-75
Human Comedy, The, $100-150
Hunt for Red October, The, $30-40
Hurricane, The, $250-300
Hustler, The, $200-250
I am a Promise (Color 8 x 10" still), $20-25
I Want to Live, $75-100
I Wanted Wings, $100-150
I'll Cry Tomorrow, $50-75
In Beaver Valley (One-sheet), $200-250
In Old Arizona, $250-300
In Old Chicago, $300-400
In the Heat of the Night, $75-100
In Which We Serve, $150-200
Independence Day, $30-40
Indiana Jones and the Last Crusade, $40-50
Indiana Jones and the Temple of Doom, $40-50
Indochine (One-sheet), $100-150
Informer, The, $400-500
Innerspace (One-sheet), $30-40
Interrupted Melody, $75-100
Invaders, The, $250-300
Investigation of a Citizen Above Suspicion, $40-60
Iris (Press Release), $10-15
Irma La Douce, $50-75
It Happened One Night, $800-1000
It's A Mad, Mad, Mad, Mad World, $100-150
Jacques-Yves Cousteau's World Without Sun, $100-125
Jaws, $100-125
Jazz Singer, The, $2500-3000
Jerry Maguire, $30-40
Jezebel, $500-600
JFK (Color 8 x 10" still), $20-25
Joan of Arc, $150-200
Johnny Belinda, $100-150
Johnny Eager, $150-200
Joker is Wild, The, $75-100
Jolson Story, The, $100-150
Journey of Hope (8 x 10" still), $20-25
Judgement at Nurenberg, $50-75
Julia (Fonda, Hammett), $50-75
Julia (Redgrave, Fonda), $50-75
Julius Caesar, $200-250

Jurassic Park, $40-60
Kentucky, $200-250
Key Largo, $800-1000
Killing Fields, The, $40-50
King and I, The, $100-125
King Gimp (Color 8 x 10" still), $25-30
King Kong, $100-150
King of Jazz (jumbo 14 x 17"), $250-300
King Solomon's Mines, $150-200
Kiss of the Spider Woman (One-sheet), $75-100
Kitty Foyle, $150-200
Klute, $75-100
Kolya (Color 8 x 10" still), $20-25
Kon-Tiki, $100-125
Krakatoa, (One-sheet), $300-400
Kramer vs. Kramer, $50-75
Kukan, $250-300
L.A. Confidential (Spanish lobby card), $30-40
La Cucaracha, $250-300
La Dolce Vita, $100-150
La Strada, $75-100
Lady Be Good, $300-400
Last Command, The, $800-1000
Last Days, The (One-sheet), $75-100
Last Emperor, The (One-sheet), $75-100
Last of the Mohicans, The (One-sheet), $50-75
Last Picture Show, The (Half-sheet), $50-75
Laura , $350-400
Lavender Hill Mob, The, $150-200
Lawrence of Arabia, $100-125
Leave Her to Heaven, $250-300
Leaving Las Vegas (One-sheet), $75-100
Legends of the Fall, $30-40
Les Girls, $75-100
Let it Be, $150-200
Letter to Three Wives, A, $100-125
Life is Beautiful (One-sheet), $100-150
Life of Emile Zola, The, $300-400
Lili, $75-100
Lilies of the Field, $75-100
Limelight, $200-250
Lion in Winter, The, $100-125
Lion King, The, $30-40
Little Kidnappers, The, $20-30
Little Mermaid, $40-50
Little Miss Marker, $400-500
Little Night Music, A (One-sheet), $100-150
Little Romance, A, $40-60
Little Women, $150-200
Little Women, $300-400
Lives of a Bengal Lancer, The, $300-400
Living Desert, The, $50-75
Logan's Run, $75-100
Longest Day, The, $50-75
Lord of the Rings, The (British quad), $60-80
Lost Horizon, $600-800
Lost Weekend, The, $200-250
Love is a Many Splendored Thing, $75-100
Love Me or Leave Me, $150-200

Love Story, $100-125
Lovers and Other Strangers, $50-75
Lust for Life, $75-100
M*A*S*H, $100-125
Madame Rosa (One-sheet), $150-200
Madness of King George, The (One-sheet), $75-100
Man and a Woman, A, $75-100
Man For All Seasons, A, $75-100
Man Who Knew Too Much, The, $75-100
Man Who Skied Down Everest, The (One-sheet), $250-300
Manhattan Melodrama, $600-800
March of Time, The (Linen-backed one-sheet), $600-800
Marie-Louise (8 x 10" still), $25
Marjoe, $40-50
Marooned, $50-75
Marty, $50-75
Mary Poppins, $75-100
Mask, $30-40
Matrix, The, $30-40
Maya Lin: A Strong and Clear Vision (8 x 10" still), $15-20
Mediterraneo (One-sheet), $100-125
Melvin and Howard, $25-30
Men in Black, $30-40
Mephisto (One-sheet), $150-200
Merry Widow, The, $400-500
Mickey Mouse, $4000-5000
Midnight Cowboy, $100-125
Midnight Express, $40-60
Midsummer Night's Dream, A (Jumbo lobby card), $400-500
Mighty Aphrodite (One-sheet), $75-100
Mighty Joe Young, $400-500
Milagro Beanfield War, The, $30-40
Mildred Pierce, $150-200
Min and Bill, $350-400
Miracle on 34th Street, $200-250
Miracle Worker, The, $50-75
Misery, $25-50
Missing, $40-50
Mission (Brochure), $20-30
Mississippi Burning (One-sheet), $50-75
Mister Roberts, $200-250
Monsieur Vincent, $75-100
Monster's Ball (One-sheet), $25-30
Monsters, Inc. (Color 8 x 10" still), $25-30
Moonstruck, $30-40
More the Merrier, The, $250-300
Morning Glory, $400-500
Moscow Does Not Believe In Tears (8 x 10" still), $20
Moscow Strikes Back (One-sheet), $500-600
Mother Wore Tights, $100-150
Moulin Rouge, $150-200
Moulin Rouge, $25-30
Mr. Deeds Goes to Town, $400-500
Mr. Smith Goes to Washington, $400-500
Mrs. Doubtfire, $40-50
Mrs. Miniver, $150-200

Murder on the Orient Express, $150-200
Music Box, The, $1500-2000
Music Man, The, $50-75
Mutiny on the Bounty, $350-400
My Cousin Vinny, $30-40
My Fair Lady, $100-150
My Gal Sal, $250-300
My Left Foot (One-sheet), $50-75
My Uncle (Mon Oncle), $75-100
Naked City, The, $75-100
Nashville, $50-75
National Velvet, $300-400
Nature's Half Acre, $40-50
Naughty Marietta, $700-800
Neptune's Daughter, $100-150
Network, $75-100
Never on Sunday, $75-100
Nicholas and Alexandra, $75-100
Night of the Iguana, The, $100-150
Nights of Cabiria, The, $75-100
No Man's Land (One-sheet), $40-50
None But the Lonely Heart, $150-200
Norma Rae, $50-75
North West Mounted Police, $250-300
Now, Voyager, $300-400
Nutty Professor, The, $30-40
Officer and a Gentleman, An, $40-50
Official Story, The (One-sheet), $75-100
Oklahoma, $150-200
Old Man and the Sea, $75-100
Old Mill, The (8 x 10" still), $30
Oliver!, $75-100
Omen, The, $50-75
On Golden Pond, $75-100
On the Town, $150-200
On The Waterfront, $150-200
One Day in September (Color 8 x 10" still), $20-25
One Flew Over the Cukoo's Nest, $75-100
One Hundred Men and a Girl, $300-400
One Night of Love, $300-400
One Way Passage, $250-300
Ordinary People, $30-40
Out of Africa, $40-50
Paleface, The, $100-150
Panic in the Streets, $75-100
Papa'a Delicate Condition, $25-50
Paper Chase, The , $50-75
Paper Moon, $50-75
Passage to India, A, $30-40
Patch of Blue, A, $50-75
Patriot, The, $100-150
Patton, $100-125
Paul Robeson, Tribute to an Artist (8 x 10" still), $40-50
Pearl Harbor, $20-25
Pelle the Conqueror (One-sheet), $100-150
Personals, The (8 x 10" still), $15-20
Pete Smith Specialties (One-sheet, linen backed), $500-700
Phantom of the Opera, The, $400-500
Philadelphia, $40-50

Philadelphia Story, The, $800-1000
Piano, The (One-sheet), $75-100
Picnic, $75-100
Picture of Dorian Gray, The, $150-200
Pillow Talk, $100-150
Pinocchio, $700-800
Place in the Sun, A, $100-150
Places in the Heart (One-sheet), $75-100
Planet of the Apes, $75-100
Platoon, $30-40
Plymouth Adventure, $75-100
Pochahontas, $30-40
Pollock (Color 8 x 10" still), $20-25
Pollyanna, $60-75
Porgy and Bess (Mini-window card), $150-200
Portrait of Jennie, $150-200
Poseidon Adventure, The, $100-150
Postman, The (Il Postino), $40-60
Prelude to War, $150-200
Pride and Prejudice, $300-400
Pride of the Yankees, The, $250-300
Prime of Miss Jean Brody, The, $50-75
Prince of Egypt, The, $30-40
Princess O'Rourke, $150-200
Private Life of Henry VIII, The, $250-350
Prizzi's Honor, $30-40
Producers, The, $150-200
Pulp Fiction (French Lobby Card), $40-50
Purple Rain, $40-50
Pygmalion, $300-300
Quest For Fire, $30-40
Quiet Man, The, $300-400
Raging Bull, $75-100
Raiders of the Lost Ark, $75-100
Rain Man, $40-50
Rains Came, The, $200-250
Ran, $60-80
Rasho-Mon, $150-200
Razor's Edge, The, $250-300
Reap the Wild Wind, $250-300
Rebecca, $800-1000
Red Balloon, The (One-sheet), $250-300
Red Shoes, The, $200-250
Red Violin, The (Color 8 x 10" still), $25-30
Reds, $50-75
Restoration (One-sheet), $75-100
Resurrection of Broncho Billy (One-sheet), $150-200
Return of the Jedi, $75
Reversal of Fortune (One-sheet), $100-150
Right Stuff, The, $40-50
River Runs Through It, A (One-sheet), $80-100
River, The, $30-40
Robe, The, $150-200
Robocop, $40-50
Rocky, $100-150
Roman Holiday, $250-300
Romeo and Juliet, $75-100
Room at the Top, $75-100
Room With a View, A (One-sheet), $100-150
Rose Tattoo, The, $75-100

Rosemary's Baby, $75-100
Round Midnight, $30-40
Ryan's Daughter, $75-100
Sabrina, $100-150
Samson and Delilah, $100-150
San Francisco, $600-800
Sandpiper, The, $75-100
Save the Tiger, $40-60
Saving Private Ryan, $60-80
Sayonara, $50-75
Scent of a Woman, $40-50
Schindler's List, $75-100
Scoundrel, The, $250-300
Sea Around Us, The, $75-100
Seal Island, $150-200
Search, The, $75-100
Secret Land, The (One-sheet), $300-400
Sense and Sensibility (One-sheet), $75-100
Separate Tables (Hayworth/Hiller), $75-100
Separate Tables (Niven), $75-100
Serengeti Shall Not Die, $75-100
Sergeant York, $300-400
Seven Brides for Seven Brothers, $75-100
Seven Days to Noon, $75-100
Seven Faces of Dr. Lao, $75-100
7th Heaven, $800-1000
Seventh Veil, The, $150-200
Shaft, $75-100
Shakespeare In Love, $30-40
Shampoo, $50-75
Shane, $250-300
Shanghai Express, $3000-4000
She Wore a Yellow Ribbon, $300-400
Shine (One-sheet), $75-100
Ship of Fools, $25-50
Shoe Shine (8 x 10" still), $30
Shop on the Main Street, The, $50-75
Shrek, $30-40
Silence of the Lambs (Foster), $40-50
Silence of the Lambs (Hopkins)(French lobby card), $40-50
Silent World, The, $100-150
Sin of Madelon Claudet, The, $200-250
Since You Went Away, $200-250
Skippy, $200-250
Sky Above and Mud Beneath, $50-75
Sleepy Hollow, $30-40
Sling Blade (One-sheet), $75-100
Snake Pit, The, $150-200
Snow White and the Seven Dwarfs, $700-800
So This is Harris (8 x 10" still), $20
Solid Gold Cadillac, The, $50-75
Some Like it Hot, $300-400
Somebody Up There Likes Me, $75-100
Song of Bernadette, The, $200-250
Song of the South, $150-200
Song Without End, $50-75
Sons and Lovers, $50-75
Sons of Liberty, $150-200
Sophie's Choice, $40-50
Sound of Music, The, $100-150
South Pacific, $75-100

Spartacus, $100-150
Spawn of the North, $250-300
Speaking of Animals and Their Families (One-sheet), $300-400
Speed (Flyer), $10-20
Spellbound, $600-800
Splendor in the Grass, $75-100
Stagecoach, $2500-3000
Stalag 17, $150-200
Star is Born, A, $50-75
Star Is Born, A, $300-400
Star Wars, $100-150
State Fair, $200-250
Sting, The, $100-150
Story of Louis Pasteur, The, $300-400
Stratton Story, The, $75-100
Street Angel, $400-500
Streetcar Named Desire, A, $100-125
Strike Up the Band, $300-400
Subject was Roses, The, $50-75
Summer of '42, $75-100
Sundays and Cybele, $75-100
Sunrise, $1200-1500
Sunset Boulevard, $400-500
Sunshine Boys, The, $50-75
Superman, $60-80
Sweet Bird of Youth, $50-75
Sweethearts, $250-300
Swing Time, $600-800
Tabu, $1200-1500
Target For Tonight (One-sheet), $150-200
Tarzan, $30-40
Teddy, The Rough Rider (Linen-lined one-sheet), $800-1000
Tempest, The, $400-500
Ten Commandments, The, $100-125
Tender Mercies, $30-40
Terminator 2: Judgement Day, $40-60
Terms of Endearment, $40-50
Tess (French lobby card), $50-75
Thank God It's Friday, $40-60
That Hamilton Woman, $300-400
Their Own Desire, $400-500
Thelma and Louise, $40-50
They Shoot Horses Don't They?, $50-75
Thief of Bagdad, The, $300-400
Third Man, The, $250-300
Thirty Seconds Over Tokyo, $200-250
This Above All, $200-250
This is the Army, $250-300
This Land is Mine, $150-200
Thomas Crown Affair, The, $75-100
Thoroughly Modern Mille, $75-100
Thousand Clowns, A (8 x 10" still), $20-25
Three Coins in the Fountain, $100-125
Three Faces of Eve, The, $50-75
Three Little Pigs, The, $150-200
Three Orphan Kittens (8 x 10" still), $30
Through a Glass Darkly, $75-100
Thunderball, $150-200
Time Machine, The, $300-400
Times of Harvey Milk, The (8 x 10" still), $20-25

Tin Drum, The (Spanish one-sheet), $100-150
Tin Pan Alley, $250-300
Titan: Story of Michelangelo, The (8 x 10" still), $20
Titanic, $100-150
Titanic (One-sheet), $60-75
To Catch a Thief, $200-250
To Each His Own, $100-150
To Kill a Mockingbird, $100-125
Tom Jones, $50-75
Tom Thumb, $50-75
Tootsie, $40-50
Top Gun, $50-75
Topkapi, $75-100
Topsy-Turvy (Color 8 x 10" still), $25-30
Tora! Tora! Tora! (Spanish one-sheet), $100-150
Tortoise and the Hare, The (8 x 10" still), $30
Torture Money (8 x 10" still), $10
Total Recall, $30-40
Touch of Class, A, $50-75
Towering Inferno, The (British quad), $200-250
Toy Story, $30-40
Traffic (One-sheet), $50-75
Training Day (One-sheet), $25-30
Transatlantic, $150-200
Travels With My Aunt, $50-75
Treasure of the Sierra Madre, The, $1200-1500
Tree Grows in Brooklyn, A, $150-200
Trevor (8 x 10" still), $15-20
Trip to Bountiful, The (8 x 10" still), $20-25
True Glory, The, $150-200
True Grit, $100-125
12 O'Clock High, $100-125
20,000 Leagues Under the Sea, $100-150
Two Arabian Nights, $200-500
2001: A Space Odyssey, $100-125
Two Women, $75-100
U-571 (Color 8 x 10" still), $25-30
Ugly Duckling, The, $200-250
Underworld, $400-500
Unforgiven (German one-sheet), $100-150
Untouchables, The, $60-80
Usual Suspects, The (Color 8 x 10" still), $20-25
Vacation From Marriage, $150-200
Vanishing Prairie, The, $40-50
Victor / Victoria, $40-50
V.I.P.s, The, $40-50
Virgin Spring, The, $150-200
Viva Villa!, $250-300
Viva Zapata!, $150-200
Waikiki Wedding, $250-300
Wall Street, $75-100
Walls of Malapaga, The (8 x 10" still), $25
War and Peace, $75-100
War Game, The, (One-sheet), $75-100
War of the Worlds, The, $200-250
Watch on the Rhine, $250-300
Water Birds, $75-100

Way of All Flesh, Way, $400-500
Way We Were, The, $75-100
West Side Story (Chakiris), $50-75
West Side Story (Moreno), $50-75
Westerner, The, $300-400
Wetback Hound, The (8 x 10" still), $10-15
What Dreams May Come (One-sheet), $40-50
What Ever Happened to Baby Jane?, $100-150
When Magoo Flew (One-sheet, linen-backed), $600-800
When Tomorrow Comes, $300-400
When We Were Kings (Color 8 x 10" still), $30-40
When Worlds Collide, $150-20
White Nights, $30-40
White Shadows in the South Seas, $200-250
White Wilderness, $50-75
Who Framed Roger Rabbit?, $40-50
Who's Afraid of Virginia Woolf ?, $75-100
Wilson, $150-200
Wings, $400-500
Winnie The Pooh and the Blustery Day, $75-100
With a Song in my Heart, $75-100
With Byrd at the South Pole, $500-600
With the Marines at Tarawa, $150-200
Witness, $30-40
Wizard of Oz, The, $4000-5000
Woman in Red, The, $40-50
Woman of the Year, $300-400
Women in Love, $50-75
Wonder Boys (One-sheet), $30-40
Wonder Man, $150-200
Wonderful World of the Brothers Grimm, $50-75
Woodstock, $100-125
Working Girl, $50-75
Written on the Wind, $75-100
Wrong Trousers, The (8 x 10" still), $15-20
Wuthering Heights, $600-800
Yankee Doodle Dandy, $300-400
Yearling, The, $150-200
Year of Living Dangerously, The (Spanish lobby card), $30-40
Yentl, $30-40
Yesterday, Today and Tomorrow, $100-125
You Can't Take it With You, $800-1000
You Light up my Life, $25-50
Young at Heart (8 x 10" still), $20-25
Z, $100-125
Zorba, The Greek, $100-150

INDEX

309

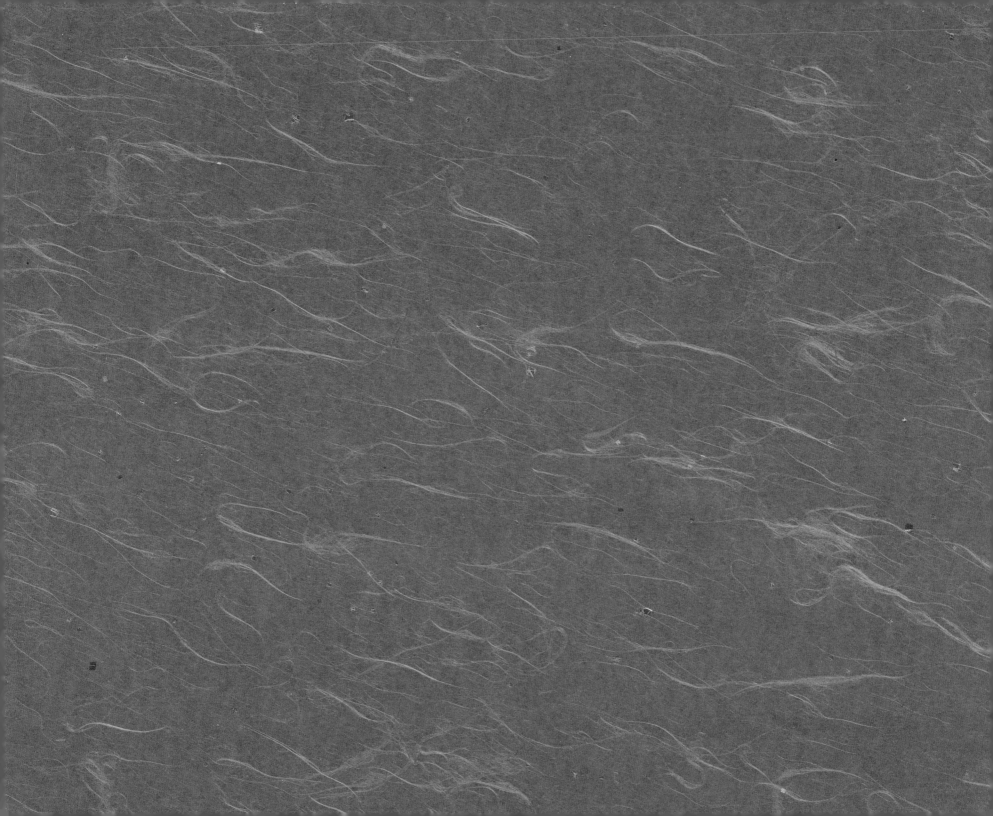